The Book Lover's Journal

My Personal Reading Record

BY RENE J. SMITH

 PETER PAUPER PRESS, INC.
WHITE PLAINS, NEW YORK

PETER PAUPER PRESS
Fine Books and Gifts Since 1928

Our Company

In 1928, at the age of twenty-two, Peter Beilenson began printing books on a small press in the basement of his parents' home in Larchmont, New York. Peter—and later, his wife, Edna—sought to create fine books that sold at "prices even a pauper could afford."

Today, still family owned and operated, Peter Pauper Press continues to honor our founders' legacy—and our customers' expectations—of beauty, quality, and value.

All good books are alike in that they are truer than if they really happened and after you are finished reading one you will feel that it all happened to you, and afterwards it all belongs to you.

ERNEST HEMINGWAY

Designed by Margaret Rubiano

Illustrations: Canicula/Shutterstock, Trucic/Shutterstock

Copyright © 2017
Peter Pauper Press, Inc.
202 Mamaroneck Avenue
White Plains, NY 10601
All rights reserved
ISBN 978-1-4413-0482-7
Printed in Hong Kong
21 20 19 18

Visit us at www.peterpauper.com

CONTENTS

INTRODUCTION 5

MY BOOK LOG 7
Pages turned

BOOKS I'D LIKE TO READ 145
My reading wish list

MY BOOKS 169
Books bought, borrowed, lent, and given

BOOK GROUP INFO 185
Friends and fellow readers

ACCLAIMED AUTHORS AND BOOKS 193
Inspiration for future reading

MY READING LIFE 201
My life with books

*A good book is the best of friends,
the same today and forever.*

MARTIN F. TUPPER

INTRODUCTION

What do you want to read today? A riveting mystery? A compelling biography? A fact-packed historical account? A literary classic? No matter what you choose, read it and record it. Your book may make you laugh or cry, feel angry, inspired, or simply better informed. Write down your reactions in your *Book Lover's Journal*.

Months and years from now, this journal will help you instantly recall long-forgotten details of your reading experience. This is also the place to record books you'd like to read next (take it with you to the book-store or library). You'll find pages to list books borrowed or lent, book sources and book group contact information, lists of acclaimed authors and titles to inspire future reading choices, and a section devoted to your reading life.

*If we encounter a man
of rare intellect, we should ask
him what books he reads.*

RALPH WALDO EMERSON

MY BOOK LOG
Pages turned

Keep a record of books as you read them in this
main section. Each book gets a two-page
spread. Fill in the specifics for each book, rate
and review it, and record your own notes and
thoughts about the book.

Use the next two pages (pages 8 and 9) as your
own "Table of Contents" for this section of the
Journal. Write down the book title and the page
on which your log entry occurs. This will enable
you to find a specific book record more easily.

My Book Log *Table of Contents*

TITLE   **Journal page number**

BOOK TITLE:

Author:

Publisher:

Number of pages:

Fiction ☐ Genre:

Nonfiction ☐ Subject:

How I discovered or acquired this book:

When & where read:

Noteworthy experiences while reading this book:

Check out author's other books? ☐ Or related books? ☐
(If yes, add them to **Books I'd Like to Read**—see page 145.)

Rate on a scale of 1 to 10 (10 being exceptional):

Quality of writing	1	2	3	4	5	6	7	8	9	10	NA
Pace	1	2	3	4	5	6	7	8	9	10	NA
Plot development	1	2	3	4	5	6	7	8	9	10	NA
Characters	1	2	3	4	5	6	7	8	9	10	NA
Enjoyability	1	2	3	4	5	6	7	8	9	10	NA
Insightfulness	1	2	3	4	5	6	7	8	9	10	NA
Ease of reading	1	2	3	4	5	6	7	8	9	10	NA
Photos/Illustrations	1	2	3	4	5	6	7	8	9	10	NA

Recommend this book? ☐ To whom?

NOTES AND OPINIONS:

Basic plot or contents, setting, main characters, point of view, how this book made me feel or what it made me think, great lines or quotes, etc.

Overall rating: ☆☆☆☆☆

BOOK TITLE:

Author:

Publisher:

Number of pages:

Fiction ☐ Genre:

Nonfiction ☐ Subject:

How I discovered or acquired this book:

When & where read:

Noteworthy experiences while reading this book:

Check out author's other books? ☐ Or related books? ☐
(If yes, add them to **Books I'd Like to Read**—see page 145.)

Rate on a scale of 1 to 10 (10 being exceptional):

Quality of writing	1	2	3	4	5	6	7	8	9	10	NA
Pace	1	2	3	4	5	6	7	8	9	10	NA
Plot development	1	2	3	4	5	6	7	8	9	10	NA
Characters	1	2	3	4	5	6	7	8	9	10	NA
Enjoyability	1	2	3	4	5	6	7	8	9	10	NA
Insightfulness	1	2	3	4	5	6	7	8	9	10	NA
Ease of reading	1	2	3	4	5	6	7	8	9	10	NA
Photos/Illustrations	1	2	3	4	5	6	7	8	9	10	NA

Recommend this book? ☐ To whom?

NOTES AND OPINIONS:
Basic plot or contents, setting, main characters, point of view, how this book made me feel or what it made me think, great lines or quotes, etc.

Overall rating: ☆☆☆☆☆

BOOK TITLE:

Author:

Publisher:

Number of pages:

Fiction ☐ Genre:

Nonfiction ☐ Subject:

How I discovered or acquired this book:

When & where read:

Noteworthy experiences while reading this book:

Check out author's other books? ☐ Or related books? ☐
(If yes, add them to **Books I'd Like to Read**—see page 145.)

Rate on a scale of 1 to 10 (10 being exceptional):

Quality of writing	1	2	3	4	5	6	7	8	9	10	NA
Pace	1	2	3	4	5	6	7	8	9	10	NA
Plot development	1	2	3	4	5	6	7	8	9	10	NA
Characters	1	2	3	4	5	6	7	8	9	10	NA
Enjoyability	1	2	3	4	5	6	7	8	9	10	NA
Insightfulness	1	2	3	4	5	6	7	8	9	10	NA
Ease of reading	1	2	3	4	5	6	7	8	9	10	NA
Photos/Illustrations	1	2	3	4	5	6	7	8	9	10	NA

Recommend this book? ☐ To whom?

NOTES AND OPINIONS:

Basic plot or contents, setting, main characters, point of view, how this book made me feel or what it made me think, great lines or quotes, etc.

Overall rating: ☆☆☆☆☆

BOOK TITLE:

Author:

Publisher:

Number of pages:

Fiction ☐ Genre:

Nonfiction ☐ Subject:

How I discovered or acquired this book:

When & where read:

Noteworthy experiences while reading this book:

Check out author's other books? ☐ Or related books? ☐
(If yes, add them to **Books I'd Like to Read**—see page 145.)

Rate on a scale of 1 to 10 (10 being exceptional):

Quality of writing	1	2	3	4	5	6	7	8	9	10	NA
Pace	1	2	3	4	5	6	7	8	9	10	NA
Plot development	1	2	3	4	5	6	7	8	9	10	NA
Characters	1	2	3	4	5	6	7	8	9	10	NA
Enjoyability	1	2	3	4	5	6	7	8	9	10	NA
Insightfulness	1	2	3	4	5	6	7	8	9	10	NA
Ease of reading	1	2	3	4	5	6	7	8	9	10	NA
Photos/Illustrations	1	2	3	4	5	6	7	8	9	10	NA

Recommend this book? ☐ To whom?

NOTES AND OPINIONS:

Basic plot or contents, setting, main characters, point of view, how this book made me feel or what it made me think, great lines or quotes, etc.

_____

_____

_____

_____

_____

_____

_____

_____

_____

_____

_____

_____

_____

_____

_____

_____

_____

_____

_____

_____

_____

Overall rating: ☆☆☆☆☆

BOOK TITLE:

Author:

Publisher:

Number of pages:

Fiction ☐ Genre:

Nonfiction ☐ Subject:

How I discovered or acquired this book:

When & where read:

Noteworthy experiences while reading this book:

Check out author's other books? ☐ Or related books? ☐
(If yes, add them to **Books I'd Like to Read**—see page 145.)

Rate on a scale of 1 to 10 (10 being exceptional):

Quality of writing	1	2	3	4	5	6	7	8	9	10	NA
Pace	1	2	3	4	5	6	7	8	9	10	NA
Plot development	1	2	3	4	5	6	7	8	9	10	NA
Characters	1	2	3	4	5	6	7	8	9	10	NA
Enjoyability	1	2	3	4	5	6	7	8	9	10	NA
Insightfulness	1	2	3	4	5	6	7	8	9	10	NA
Ease of reading	1	2	3	4	5	6	7	8	9	10	NA
Photos/Illustrations	1	2	3	4	5	6	7	8	9	10	NA

Recommend this book? ☐ To whom?

NOTES AND OPINIONS:

Basic plot or contents, setting, main characters, point of view, how this book made me feel or what it made me think, great lines or quotes, etc.

Overall rating: ☆☆☆☆☆

BOOK TITLE:

Author:

Publisher:

Number of pages:

Fiction ☐ Genre:

Nonfiction ☐ Subject:

How I discovered or acquired this book:

When & where read:

Noteworthy experiences while reading this book:

Check out author's other books? ☐ Or related books? ☐
(If yes, add them to **Books I'd Like to Read**—see page 145.)

Rate on a scale of 1 to 10 (10 being exceptional):

Quality of writing	1	2	3	4	5	6	7	8	9	10	NA
Pace	1	2	3	4	5	6	7	8	9	10	NA
Plot development	1	2	3	4	5	6	7	8	9	10	NA
Characters	1	2	3	4	5	6	7	8	9	10	NA
Enjoyability	1	2	3	4	5	6	7	8	9	10	NA
Insightfulness	1	2	3	4	5	6	7	8	9	10	NA
Ease of reading	1	2	3	4	5	6	7	8	9	10	NA
Photos/Illustrations	1	2	3	4	5	6	7	8	9	10	NA

Recommend this book? ☐ To whom?

NOTES AND OPINIONS:
Basic plot or contents, setting, main characters, point of view, how this book made me feel or what it made me think, great lines or quotes, etc.

_____

_____

_____

_____

_____

_____

_____

_____

_____

_____

_____

_____

_____

_____

_____

_____

_____

_____

_____

_____

_____

_____

_____

_____

Overall rating: ☆☆☆☆☆

BOOK TITLE:

Author:

Publisher:

Number of pages:

Fiction ☐ Genre:

Nonfiction ☐ Subject:

How I discovered or acquired this book:

When & where read:

Noteworthy experiences while reading this book:

Check out author's other books? ☐ Or related books? ☐
(If yes, add them to **Books I'd Like to Read**—see page 145.)

Rate on a scale of 1 to 10 (10 being exceptional):

Quality of writing	1	2	3	4	5	6	7	8	9	10	NA
Pace	1	2	3	4	5	6	7	8	9	10	NA
Plot development	1	2	3	4	5	6	7	8	9	10	NA
Characters	1	2	3	4	5	6	7	8	9	10	NA
Enjoyability	1	2	3	4	5	6	7	8	9	10	NA
Insightfulness	1	2	3	4	5	6	7	8	9	10	NA
Ease of reading	1	2	3	4	5	6	7	8	9	10	NA
Photos/Illustrations	1	2	3	4	5	6	7	8	9	10	NA

Recommend this book? ☐ To whom?

NOTES AND OPINIONS:

Basic plot or contents, setting, main characters, point of view, how this book made me feel or what it made me think, great lines or quotes, etc.

....

....

....

....

....

....

....

....

....

....

....

....

....

....

....

....

....

....

....

....

Overall rating: ☆☆☆☆☆

BOOK TITLE:

Author:

Publisher:

Number of pages:

Fiction ☐ Genre:

Nonfiction ☐ Subject:

How I discovered or acquired this book:

When & where read:

Noteworthy experiences while reading this book:

Check out author's other books? ☐ Or related books? ☐
(If yes, add them to **Books I'd Like to Read**—see page 145.)

Rate on a scale of 1 to 10 (10 being exceptional):

Quality of writing	1	2	3	4	5	6	7	8	9	10	NA
Pace	1	2	3	4	5	6	7	8	9	10	NA
Plot development	1	2	3	4	5	6	7	8	9	10	NA
Characters	1	2	3	4	5	6	7	8	9	10	NA
Enjoyability	1	2	3	4	5	6	7	8	9	10	NA
Insightfulness	1	2	3	4	5	6	7	8	9	10	NA
Ease of reading	1	2	3	4	5	6	7	8	9	10	NA
Photos/Illustrations	1	2	3	4	5	6	7	8	9	10	NA

Recommend this book? ☐ To whom?

NOTES AND OPINIONS:
Basic plot or contents, setting, main characters, point of view, how this book made me feel or what it made me think, great lines or quotes, etc.

_____

_____

_____

_____

_____

_____

_____

_____

_____

_____

_____

_____

_____

_____

_____

_____

_____

_____

_____

_____

_____

Overall rating: ☆☆☆☆☆

BOOK TITLE:

Author:

Publisher:

Number of pages:

Fiction ☐ Genre:

Nonfiction ☐ Subject:

How I discovered or acquired this book:

When & where read:

Noteworthy experiences while reading this book:

Check out author's other books? ☐ Or related books? ☐
(If yes, add them to **Books I'd Like to Read**—see page 145.)

Rate on a scale of 1 to 10 (10 being exceptional):

Quality of writing	1	2	3	4	5	6	7	8	9	10	NA
Pace	1	2	3	4	5	6	7	8	9	10	NA
Plot development	1	2	3	4	5	6	7	8	9	10	NA
Characters	1	2	3	4	5	6	7	8	9	10	NA
Enjoyability	1	2	3	4	5	6	7	8	9	10	NA
Insightfulness	1	2	3	4	5	6	7	8	9	10	NA
Ease of reading	1	2	3	4	5	6	7	8	9	10	NA
Photos/Illustrations	1	2	3	4	5	6	7	8	9	10	NA

Recommend this book? ☐ To whom?

NOTES AND OPINIONS:

Basic plot or contents, setting, main characters, point of view, how this book made me feel or what it made me think, great lines or quotes, etc.

Overall rating: ☆☆☆☆☆

BOOK TITLE:

Author:

Publisher:

Number of pages:

Fiction ☐ Genre:

Nonfiction ☐ Subject:

How I discovered or acquired this book:

When & where read:

Noteworthy experiences while reading this book:

Check out author's other books? ☐ Or related books? ☐
(If yes, add them to **Books I'd Like to Read**—see page 145.)

Rate on a scale of 1 to 10 (10 being exceptional):

Quality of writing	1	2	3	4	5	6	7	8	9	10	NA
Pace	1	2	3	4	5	6	7	8	9	10	NA
Plot development	1	2	3	4	5	6	7	8	9	10	NA
Characters	1	2	3	4	5	6	7	8	9	10	NA
Enjoyability	1	2	3	4	5	6	7	8	9	10	NA
Insightfulness	1	2	3	4	5	6	7	8	9	10	NA
Ease of reading	1	2	3	4	5	6	7	8	9	10	NA
Photos/Illustrations	1	2	3	4	5	6	7	8	9	10	NA

Recommend this book? ☐ To whom?

NOTES AND OPINIONS:

Basic plot or contents, setting, main characters, point of view, how this book made me feel or what it made me think, great lines or quotes, etc.

Overall rating: ☆☆☆☆☆

BOOK TITLE:

Author:

Publisher:

Number of pages:

Fiction ☐ Genre:

Nonfiction ☐ Subject:

How I discovered or acquired this book:

When & where read:

Noteworthy experiences while reading this book:

Check out author's other books? ☐ Or related books? ☐
(If yes, add them to **Books I'd Like to Read**—see page 145.)

Rate on a scale of 1 to 10 (10 being exceptional):

Quality of writing	1	2	3	4	5	6	7	8	9	10	NA
Pace	1	2	3	4	5	6	7	8	9	10	NA
Plot development	1	2	3	4	5	6	7	8	9	10	NA
Characters	1	2	3	4	5	6	7	8	9	10	NA
Enjoyability	1	2	3	4	5	6	7	8	9	10	NA
Insightfulness	1	2	3	4	5	6	7	8	9	10	NA
Ease of reading	1	2	3	4	5	6	7	8	9	10	NA
Photos/Illustrations	1	2	3	4	5	6	7	8	9	10	NA

Recommend this book? ☐ To whom?

NOTES AND OPINIONS:

Basic plot or contents, setting, main characters, point of view, how this book made me feel or what it made me think, great lines or quotes, etc.

_____

_____

_____

_____

_____

_____

_____

_____

_____

_____

_____

_____

_____

_____

_____

_____

_____

_____

_____

_____

_____

_____

Overall rating: ☆☆☆☆☆

BOOK TITLE:

Author:

Publisher:

Number of pages:

Fiction ☐ **Genre:**

Nonfiction ☐ **Subject:**

How I discovered or acquired this book:

When & where read:

Noteworthy experiences while reading this book:

Check out author's other books? ☐ Or related books? ☐
(If yes, add them to **Books I'd Like to Read**—see page 145.)

Rate on a scale of 1 to 10 (10 being exceptional):

Quality of writing	1	2	3	4	5	6	7	8	9	10	NA
Pace	1	2	3	4	5	6	7	8	9	10	NA
Plot development	1	2	3	4	5	6	7	8	9	10	NA
Characters	1	2	3	4	5	6	7	8	9	10	NA
Enjoyability	1	2	3	4	5	6	7	8	9	10	NA
Insightfulness	1	2	3	4	5	6	7	8	9	10	NA
Ease of reading	1	2	3	4	5	6	7	8	9	10	NA
Photos/Illustrations	1	2	3	4	5	6	7	8	9	10	NA

Recommend this book? ☐ To whom?

NOTES AND OPINIONS:
Basic plot or contents, setting, main characters, point of view, how this book made me feel or what it made me think, great lines or quotes, etc.

_____

_____

_____

_____

_____

_____

_____

_____

_____

_____

_____

_____

_____

_____

_____

_____

_____

_____

_____

_____

Overall rating: ☆☆☆☆☆

BOOK TITLE:

Author:

Publisher:

Number of pages:

Fiction ☐ Genre:

Nonfiction ☐ Subject:

How I discovered or acquired this book:

When & where read:

Noteworthy experiences while reading this book:

Check out author's other books? ☐ Or related books? ☐
(If yes, add them to **Books I'd Like to Read**—see page 145.)

Rate on a scale of 1 to 10 (10 being exceptional):

Quality of writing	1	2	3	4	5	6	7	8	9	10	NA
Pace	1	2	3	4	5	6	7	8	9	10	NA
Plot development	1	2	3	4	5	6	7	8	9	10	NA
Characters	1	2	3	4	5	6	7	8	9	10	NA
Enjoyability	1	2	3	4	5	6	7	8	9	10	NA
Insightfulness	1	2	3	4	5	6	7	8	9	10	NA
Ease of reading	1	2	3	4	5	6	7	8	9	10	NA
Photos/Illustrations	1	2	3	4	5	6	7	8	9	10	NA

Recommend this book? ☐ To whom?

NOTES AND OPINIONS:
Basic plot or contents, setting, main characters, point of view, how this book made me feel or what it made me think, great lines or quotes, etc.

_____

_____

_____

_____

_____

_____

_____

_____

_____

_____

_____

_____

_____

_____

_____

_____

_____

_____

_____

_____

_____

Overall rating: ☆☆☆☆☆

BOOK TITLE:

Author:

Publisher:

Number of pages:

Fiction ☐ Genre:

Nonfiction ☐ Subject:

How I discovered or acquired this book:

When & where read:

Noteworthy experiences while reading this book:

Check out author's other books? ☐ Or related books? ☐
(If yes, add them to **Books I'd Like to Read**—see page 145.)

Rate on a scale of 1 to 10 (10 being exceptional):

Quality of writing	1	2	3	4	5	6	7	8	9	10	NA
Pace	1	2	3	4	5	6	7	8	9	10	NA
Plot development	1	2	3	4	5	6	7	8	9	10	NA
Characters	1	2	3	4	5	6	7	8	9	10	NA
Enjoyability	1	2	3	4	5	6	7	8	9	10	NA
Insightfulness	1	2	3	4	5	6	7	8	9	10	NA
Ease of reading	1	2	3	4	5	6	7	8	9	10	NA
Photos/Illustrations	1	2	3	4	5	6	7	8	9	10	NA

Recommend this book? ☐ To whom?

NOTES AND OPINIONS:
Basic plot or contents, setting, main characters, point of view, how this book made me feel or what it made me think, great lines or quotes, etc.

Overall rating: ☆☆☆☆☆

BOOK TITLE:

Author:

Publisher:

Number of pages:

Fiction ☐ Genre:

Nonfiction ☐ Subject:

How I discovered or acquired this book:

When & where read:

Noteworthy experiences while reading this book:

Check out author's other books? ☐ Or related books? ☐
(If yes, add them to **Books I'd Like to Read**—see page 145.)

Rate on a scale of 1 to 10 (10 being exceptional):

Quality of writing	1	2	3	4	5	6	7	8	9	10	NA
Pace	1	2	3	4	5	6	7	8	9	10	NA
Plot development	1	2	3	4	5	6	7	8	9	10	NA
Characters	1	2	3	4	5	6	7	8	9	10	NA
Enjoyability	1	2	3	4	5	6	7	8	9	10	NA
Insightfulness	1	2	3	4	5	6	7	8	9	10	NA
Ease of reading	1	2	3	4	5	6	7	8	9	10	NA
Photos/Illustrations	1	2	3	4	5	6	7	8	9	10	NA

Recommend this book? ☐ To whom?

NOTES AND OPINIONS:

Basic plot or contents, setting, main characters, point of view, how this book made me feel or what it made me think, great lines or quotes, etc.

_____

_____

_____

_____

_____

_____

_____

_____

_____

_____

_____

_____

_____

_____

_____

_____

_____

_____

_____

_____

Overall rating: ☆☆☆☆☆

BOOK TITLE:

Author:

Publisher:

Number of pages:

Fiction ☐ Genre:

Nonfiction ☐ Subject:

How I discovered or acquired this book:

When & where read:

Noteworthy experiences while reading this book:

Check out author's other books? ☐ Or related books? ☐
(If yes, add them to **Books I'd Like to Read**–see page 145.)

Rate on a scale of 1 to 10 (10 being exceptional):

Quality of writing	1	2	3	4	5	6	7	8	9	10	NA
Pace	1	2	3	4	5	6	7	8	9	10	NA
Plot development	1	2	3	4	5	6	7	8	9	10	NA
Characters	1	2	3	4	5	6	7	8	9	10	NA
Enjoyability	1	2	3	4	5	6	7	8	9	10	NA
Insightfulness	1	2	3	4	5	6	7	8	9	10	NA
Ease of reading	1	2	3	4	5	6	7	8	9	10	NA
Photos/Illustrations	1	2	3	4	5	6	7	8	9	10	NA

Recommend this book? ☐ To whom?

NOTES AND OPINIONS:

Basic plot or contents, setting, main characters, point of view, how this book made me feel or what it made me think, great lines or quotes, etc.

....

....

....

....

....

....

....

....

....

....

....

....

....

....

....

....

....

....

....

....

Overall rating: ☆☆☆☆☆

BOOK TITLE:

Author:

Publisher:

Number of pages:

Fiction ☐ Genre:

Nonfiction ☐ Subject:

How I discovered or acquired this book:

When & where read:

Noteworthy experiences while reading this book:

Check out author's other books? ☐ Or related books? ☐
(If yes, add them to **Books I'd Like to Read**—see page 145.)

Rate on a scale of 1 to 10 (10 being exceptional):

Quality of writing	1	2	3	4	5	6	7	8	9	10	NA
Pace	1	2	3	4	5	6	7	8	9	10	NA
Plot development	1	2	3	4	5	6	7	8	9	10	NA
Characters	1	2	3	4	5	6	7	8	9	10	NA
Enjoyability	1	2	3	4	5	6	7	8	9	10	NA
Insightfulness	1	2	3	4	5	6	7	8	9	10	NA
Ease of reading	1	2	3	4	5	6	7	8	9	10	NA
Photos/Illustrations	1	2	3	4	5	6	7	8	9	10	NA

Recommend this book? ☐ To whom?

NOTES AND OPINIONS:

Basic plot or contents, setting, main characters, point of view, how this book made me feel or what it made me think, great lines or quotes, etc.

Overall rating: ☆☆☆☆☆

BOOK TITLE:

Author:

Publisher:

Number of pages:

Fiction ☐ Genre:

Nonfiction ☐ Subject:

How I discovered or acquired this book:

When & where read:

Noteworthy experiences while reading this book:

Check out author's other books? ☐ Or related books? ☐
(If yes, add them to **Books I'd Like to Read**—see page 145.)

Rate on a scale of 1 to 10 (10 being exceptional):

Quality of writing	1	2	3	4	5	6	7	8	9	10	NA
Pace	1	2	3	4	5	6	7	8	9	10	NA
Plot development	1	2	3	4	5	6	7	8	9	10	NA
Characters	1	2	3	4	5	6	7	8	9	10	NA
Enjoyability	1	2	3	4	5	6	7	8	9	10	NA
Insightfulness	1	2	3	4	5	6	7	8	9	10	NA
Ease of reading	1	2	3	4	5	6	7	8	9	10	NA
Photos/Illustrations	1	2	3	4	5	6	7	8	9	10	NA

Recommend this book? ☐ To whom?

NOTES AND OPINIONS:

Basic plot or contents, setting, main characters, point of view, how this book made me feel or what it made me think, great lines or quotes, etc.

Overall rating: ☆☆☆☆☆

BOOK TITLE:

Author:

Publisher:

Number of pages:

Fiction ☐ Genre:

Nonfiction ☐ Subject:

How I discovered or acquired this book:

When & where read:

Noteworthy experiences while reading this book:

Check out author's other books? ☐ Or related books? ☐
(If yes, add them to **Books I'd Like to Read**—see page 145.)

Rate on a scale of 1 to 10 (10 being exceptional):

Quality of writing	1	2	3	4	5	6	7	8	9	10	NA
Pace	1	2	3	4	5	6	7	8	9	10	NA
Plot development	1	2	3	4	5	6	7	8	9	10	NA
Characters	1	2	3	4	5	6	7	8	9	10	NA
Enjoyability	1	2	3	4	5	6	7	8	9	10	NA
Insightfulness	1	2	3	4	5	6	7	8	9	10	NA
Ease of reading	1	2	3	4	5	6	7	8	9	10	NA
Photos/Illustrations	1	2	3	4	5	6	7	8	9	10	NA

Recommend this book? ☐ To whom?

NOTES AND OPINIONS:

Basic plot or contents, setting, main characters, point of view, how this book made me feel or what it made me think, great lines or quotes, etc.

....

....

....

....

....

....

....

....

....

....

....

....

....

....

....

....

....

....

....

....

....

Overall rating: ☆☆☆☆☆

BOOK TITLE:

Author:

Publisher:

Number of pages:

Fiction ☐ Genre:

Nonfiction ☐ Subject:

How I discovered or acquired this book:

When & where read:

Noteworthy experiences while reading this book:

Check out author's other books? ☐ Or related books? ☐
(If yes, add them to **Books I'd Like to Read**—see page 145.)

Rate on a scale of 1 to 10 (10 being exceptional):

Quality of writing	1	2	3	4	5	6	7	8	9	10	NA
Pace	1	2	3	4	5	6	7	8	9	10	NA
Plot development	1	2	3	4	5	6	7	8	9	10	NA
Characters	1	2	3	4	5	6	7	8	9	10	NA
Enjoyability	1	2	3	4	5	6	7	8	9	10	NA
Insightfulness	1	2	3	4	5	6	7	8	9	10	NA
Ease of reading	1	2	3	4	5	6	7	8	9	10	NA
Photos/Illustrations	1	2	3	4	5	6	7	8	9	10	NA

Recommend this book? ☐ To whom?

NOTES AND OPINIONS:

Basic plot or contents, setting, main characters, point of view, how this book made me feel or what it made me think, great lines or quotes, etc.

Overall rating: ☆☆☆☆☆

BOOK TITLE:

Author:

Publisher:

Number of pages:

Fiction ☐ Genre:

Nonfiction ☐ Subject:

How I discovered or acquired this book:

When & where read:

Noteworthy experiences while reading this book:

Check out author's other books? ☐ Or related books? ☐
(If yes, add them to **Books I'd Like to Read**—see page 145.)

Rate on a scale of 1 to 10 (10 being exceptional):

Quality of writing	1	2	3	4	5	6	7	8	9	10	NA
Pace	1	2	3	4	5	6	7	8	9	10	NA
Plot development	1	2	3	4	5	6	7	8	9	10	NA
Characters	1	2	3	4	5	6	7	8	9	10	NA
Enjoyability	1	2	3	4	5	6	7	8	9	10	NA
Insightfulness	1	2	3	4	5	6	7	8	9	10	NA
Ease of reading	1	2	3	4	5	6	7	8	9	10	NA
Photos/Illustrations	1	2	3	4	5	6	7	8	9	10	NA

Recommend this book? ☐ To whom?

NOTES AND OPINIONS:

Basic plot or contents, setting, main characters, point of view, how this book made me feel or what it made me think, great lines or quotes, etc.

Overall rating: ☆☆☆☆☆

BOOK TITLE:

Author:

Publisher:

Number of pages:

Fiction ☐ Genre:

Nonfiction ☐ Subject:

How I discovered or acquired this book:

When & where read:

Noteworthy experiences while reading this book:

Check out author's other books? ☐ Or related books? ☐
(If yes, add them to **Books I'd Like to Read**—see page 145.)

Rate on a scale of 1 to 10 (10 being exceptional):

Quality of writing	1	2	3	4	5	6	7	8	9	10	NA
Pace	1	2	3	4	5	6	7	8	9	10	NA
Plot development	1	2	3	4	5	6	7	8	9	10	NA
Characters	1	2	3	4	5	6	7	8	9	10	NA
Enjoyability	1	2	3	4	5	6	7	8	9	10	NA
Insightfulness	1	2	3	4	5	6	7	8	9	10	NA
Ease of reading	1	2	3	4	5	6	7	8	9	10	NA
Photos/Illustrations	1	2	3	4	5	6	7	8	9	10	NA

Recommend this book? ☐ To whom?

NOTES AND OPINIONS:
Basic plot or contents, setting, main characters, point of view, how this book made me feel or what it made me think, great lines or quotes, etc.

_____

_____

_____

_____

_____

_____

_____

_____

_____

_____

_____

_____

_____

_____

_____

_____

_____

_____

_____

_____

Overall rating: ☆☆☆☆☆

BOOK TITLE:

Author:

Publisher:

Number of pages:

Fiction ☐ Genre:

Nonfiction ☐ Subject:

How I discovered or acquired this book:

When & where read:

Noteworthy experiences while reading this book:

Check out author's other books? ☐ Or related books? ☐
(If yes, add them to **Books I'd Like to Read**—see page 145.)

Rate on a scale of 1 to 10 (10 being exceptional):

Quality of writing	1	2	3	4	5	6	7	8	9	10	NA
Pace	1	2	3	4	5	6	7	8	9	10	NA
Plot development	1	2	3	4	5	6	7	8	9	10	NA
Characters	1	2	3	4	5	6	7	8	9	10	NA
Enjoyability	1	2	3	4	5	6	7	8	9	10	NA
Insightfulness	1	2	3	4	5	6	7	8	9	10	NA
Ease of reading	1	2	3	4	5	6	7	8	9	10	NA
Photos/Illustrations	1	2	3	4	5	6	7	8	9	10	NA

Recommend this book? ☐ To whom?

NOTES AND OPINIONS:

Basic plot or contents, setting, main characters, point of view, how this book made me feel or what it made me think, great lines or quotes, etc.

Overall rating: ☆☆☆☆☆

BOOK TITLE:

Author:

Publisher:

Number of pages:

Fiction ☐ Genre:

Nonfiction ☐ Subject:

How I discovered or acquired this book:

When & where read:

Noteworthy experiences while reading this book:

Check out author's other books? ☐ Or related books? ☐
(If yes, add them to **Books I'd Like to Read**—see page 145.)

Rate on a scale of 1 to 10 (10 being exceptional):

Quality of writing	1	2	3	4	5	6	7	8	9	10	NA
Pace	1	2	3	4	5	6	7	8	9	10	NA
Plot development	1	2	3	4	5	6	7	8	9	10	NA
Characters	1	2	3	4	5	6	7	8	9	10	NA
Enjoyability	1	2	3	4	5	6	7	8	9	10	NA
Insightfulness	1	2	3	4	5	6	7	8	9	10	NA
Ease of reading	1	2	3	4	5	6	7	8	9	10	NA
Photos/Illustrations	1	2	3	4	5	6	7	8	9	10	NA

Recommend this book? ☐ To whom?

NOTES AND OPINIONS:

Basic plot or contents, setting, main characters, point of view, how this book made me feel or what it made me think, great lines or quotes, etc.

Overall rating: ☆☆☆☆☆

BOOK TITLE:

Author:

Publisher:

Number of pages:

Fiction ☐ Genre:

Nonfiction ☐ Subject:

How I discovered or acquired this book:

When & where read:

Noteworthy experiences while reading this book:

Check out author's other books? ☐ Or related books? ☐
(If yes, add them to **Books I'd Like to Read**—see page 145.)

Rate on a scale of 1 to 10 (10 being exceptional):

Quality of writing	1	2	3	4	5	6	7	8	9	10	NA
Pace	1	2	3	4	5	6	7	8	9	10	NA
Plot development	1	2	3	4	5	6	7	8	9	10	NA
Characters	1	2	3	4	5	6	7	8	9	10	NA
Enjoyability	1	2	3	4	5	6	7	8	9	10	NA
Insightfulness	1	2	3	4	5	6	7	8	9	10	NA
Ease of reading	1	2	3	4	5	6	7	8	9	10	NA
Photos/Illustrations	1	2	3	4	5	6	7	8	9	10	NA

Recommend this book? ☐ To whom?

NOTES AND OPINIONS:
Basic plot or contents, setting, main characters, point of view, how this book made me feel or what it made me think, great lines or quotes, etc.

Overall rating: ☆☆☆☆☆

BOOK TITLE:

Author:

Publisher:

Number of pages:

Fiction ☐ Genre:

Nonfiction ☐ Subject:

How I discovered or acquired this book:

When & where read:

Noteworthy experiences while reading this book:

Check out author's other books? ☐ Or related books? ☐
(If yes, add them to **Books I'd Like to Read**—see page 145.)

Rate on a scale of 1 to 10 (10 being exceptional):

Quality of writing	1	2	3	4	5	6	7	8	9	10	NA
Pace	1	2	3	4	5	6	7	8	9	10	NA
Plot development	1	2	3	4	5	6	7	8	9	10	NA
Characters	1	2	3	4	5	6	7	8	9	10	NA
Enjoyability	1	2	3	4	5	6	7	8	9	10	NA
Insightfulness	1	2	3	4	5	6	7	8	9	10	NA
Ease of reading	1	2	3	4	5	6	7	8	9	10	NA
Photos/Illustrations	1	2	3	4	5	6	7	8	9	10	NA

Recommend this book? ☐ To whom?

NOTES AND OPINIONS:
Basic plot or contents, setting, main characters, point of view, how this book made me feel or what it made me think, great lines or quotes, etc.

....

....

....

....

....

....

....

....

....

....

....

....

....

....

....

....

....

....

....

....

....

Overall rating: ☆☆☆☆☆

BOOK TITLE:

Author:

Publisher:

Number of pages:

Fiction ☐ Genre:

Nonfiction ☐ Subject:

How I discovered or acquired this book:

When & where read:

Noteworthy experiences while reading this book:

Check out author's other books? ☐ Or related books? ☐
(If yes, add them to **Books I'd Like to Read**—see page 145.)

Rate on a scale of 1 to 10 (10 being exceptional):

Quality of writing	1	2	3	4	5	6	7	8	9	10	NA
Pace	1	2	3	4	5	6	7	8	9	10	NA
Plot development	1	2	3	4	5	6	7	8	9	10	NA
Characters	1	2	3	4	5	6	7	8	9	10	NA
Enjoyability	1	2	3	4	5	6	7	8	9	10	NA
Insightfulness	1	2	3	4	5	6	7	8	9	10	NA
Ease of reading	1	2	3	4	5	6	7	8	9	10	NA
Photos/Illustrations	1	2	3	4	5	6	7	8	9	10	NA

Recommend this book? ☐ To whom?

NOTES AND OPINIONS:
Basic plot or contents, setting, main characters, point of view, how this book made me feel or what it made me think, great lines or quotes, etc.

_____

_____

_____

_____

_____

_____

_____

_____

_____

_____

_____

_____

_____

_____

_____

_____

_____

_____

_____

_____

Overall rating: ☆☆☆☆☆

BOOK TITLE:

Author:

Publisher:

Number of pages:

Fiction ☐ Genre:

Nonfiction ☐ Subject:

How I discovered or acquired this book:

When & where read:

Noteworthy experiences while reading this book:

Check out author's other books? ☐ Or related books? ☐
(If yes, add them to **Books I'd Like to Read**—see page 145.)

Rate on a scale of 1 to 10 (10 being exceptional):

Quality of writing	1	2	3	4	5	6	7	8	9	10	NA
Pace	1	2	3	4	5	6	7	8	9	10	NA
Plot development	1	2	3	4	5	6	7	8	9	10	NA
Characters	1	2	3	4	5	6	7	8	9	10	NA
Enjoyability	1	2	3	4	5	6	7	8	9	10	NA
Insightfulness	1	2	3	4	5	6	7	8	9	10	NA
Ease of reading	1	2	3	4	5	6	7	8	9	10	NA
Photos/Illustrations	1	2	3	4	5	6	7	8	9	10	NA

Recommend this book? ☐ To whom?

NOTES AND OPINIONS:

Basic plot or contents, setting, main characters, point of view, how this book made me feel or what it made me think, great lines or quotes, etc.

Overall rating: ☆☆☆☆☆

BOOK TITLE:

Author:

Publisher:

Number of pages:

Fiction ☐ Genre:

Nonfiction ☐ Subject:

How I discovered or acquired this book:

When & where read:

Noteworthy experiences while reading this book:

Check out author's other books? ☐ Or related books? ☐
(If yes, add them to **Books I'd Like to Read**—see page 145.)

Rate on a scale of 1 to 10 (10 being exceptional):

Quality of writing	1	2	3	4	5	6	7	8	9	10	NA
Pace	1	2	3	4	5	6	7	8	9	10	NA
Plot development	1	2	3	4	5	6	7	8	9	10	NA
Characters	1	2	3	4	5	6	7	8	9	10	NA
Enjoyability	1	2	3	4	5	6	7	8	9	10	NA
Insightfulness	1	2	3	4	5	6	7	8	9	10	NA
Ease of reading	1	2	3	4	5	6	7	8	9	10	NA
Photos/Illustrations	1	2	3	4	5	6	7	8	9	10	NA

Recommend this book? ☐ To whom?

NOTES AND OPINIONS:

Basic plot or contents, setting, main characters, point of view, how this book made me feel or what it made me think, great lines or quotes, etc.

_____

_____

_____

_____

_____

_____

_____

_____

_____

_____

_____

_____

_____

_____

_____

_____

_____

_____

_____

_____

_____

Overall rating: ☆☆☆☆☆

BOOK TITLE:

Author:

Publisher:

Number of pages:

Fiction ☐ Genre:

Nonfiction ☐ Subject:

How I discovered or acquired this book:

When & where read:

Noteworthy experiences while reading this book:

Check out author's other books? ☐ Or related books? ☐
(If yes, add them to **Books I'd Like to Read**—see page 145.)

Rate on a scale of 1 to 10 (10 being exceptional):

Quality of writing	1	2	3	4	5	6	7	8	9	10	NA
Pace	1	2	3	4	5	6	7	8	9	10	NA
Plot development	1	2	3	4	5	6	7	8	9	10	NA
Characters	1	2	3	4	5	6	7	8	9	10	NA
Enjoyability	1	2	3	4	5	6	7	8	9	10	NA
Insightfulness	1	2	3	4	5	6	7	8	9	10	NA
Ease of reading	1	2	3	4	5	6	7	8	9	10	NA
Photos/Illustrations	1	2	3	4	5	6	7	8	9	10	NA

Recommend this book? ☐ To whom?

NOTES AND OPINIONS:

Basic plot or contents, setting, main characters, point of view, how this book made me feel or what it made me think, great lines or quotes, etc.

Overall rating: ☆☆☆☆☆

BOOK TITLE:

Author:

Publisher:

Number of pages:

Fiction ☐ Genre:

Nonfiction ☐ Subject:

How I discovered or acquired this book:

When & where read:

Noteworthy experiences while reading this book:

Check out author's other books? ☐ Or related books? ☐
(If yes, add them to **Books I'd Like to Read**—see page 145.)

Rate on a scale of 1 to 10 (10 being exceptional):

Quality of writing	1 2 3 4 5 6 7 8 9 10 NA
Pace	1 2 3 4 5 6 7 8 9 10 NA
Plot development	1 2 3 4 5 6 7 8 9 10 NA
Characters	1 2 3 4 5 6 7 8 9 10 NA
Enjoyability	1 2 3 4 5 6 7 8 9 10 NA
Insightfulness	1 2 3 4 5 6 7 8 9 10 NA
Ease of reading	1 2 3 4 5 6 7 8 9 10 NA
Photos/Illustrations	1 2 3 4 5 6 7 8 9 10 NA

Recommend this book? ☐ To whom?

NOTES AND OPINIONS:

Basic plot or contents, setting, main characters, point of view, how this book made me feel or what it made me think, great lines or quotes, etc.

_____

_____

_____

_____

_____

_____

_____

_____

_____

_____

_____

_____

_____

_____

_____

_____

_____

_____

_____

_____

Overall rating: ☆☆☆☆☆

BOOK TITLE:

Author:

Publisher:

Number of pages:

Fiction ☐ Genre:

Nonfiction ☐ Subject:

How I discovered or acquired this book:

When & where read:

Noteworthy experiences while reading this book:

Check out author's other books? ☐ Or related books? ☐
(If yes, add them to **Books I'd Like to Read**—see page 145.)

Rate on a scale of 1 to 10 (10 being exceptional):

Quality of writing	1	2	3	4	5	6	7	8	9	10	NA
Pace	1	2	3	4	5	6	7	8	9	10	NA
Plot development	1	2	3	4	5	6	7	8	9	10	NA
Characters	1	2	3	4	5	6	7	8	9	10	NA
Enjoyability	1	2	3	4	5	6	7	8	9	10	NA
Insightfulness	1	2	3	4	5	6	7	8	9	10	NA
Ease of reading	1	2	3	4	5	6	7	8	9	10	NA
Photos/Illustrations	1	2	3	4	5	6	7	8	9	10	NA

Recommend this book? ☐ To whom?

NOTES AND OPINIONS:

Basic plot or contents, setting, main characters, point of view, how this book made me feel or what it made me think, great lines or quotes, etc.

Overall rating: ☆☆☆☆☆

BOOK TITLE:

Author:

Publisher:

Number of pages:

Fiction ☐ Genre:

Nonfiction ☐ Subject:

How I discovered or acquired this book:

When & where read:

Noteworthy experiences while reading this book:

Check out author's other books? ☐ Or related books? ☐
(If yes, add them to **Books I'd Like to Read**—see page 145.)

Rate on a scale of 1 to 10 (10 being exceptional):

Quality of writing	1	2	3	4	5	6	7	8	9	10	NA
Pace	1	2	3	4	5	6	7	8	9	10	NA
Plot development	1	2	3	4	5	6	7	8	9	10	NA
Characters	1	2	3	4	5	6	7	8	9	10	NA
Enjoyability	1	2	3	4	5	6	7	8	9	10	NA
Insightfulness	1	2	3	4	5	6	7	8	9	10	NA
Ease of reading	1	2	3	4	5	6	7	8	9	10	NA
Photos/Illustrations	1	2	3	4	5	6	7	8	9	10	NA

Recommend this book? ☐ To whom?

NOTES AND OPINIONS:
Basic plot or contents, setting, main characters, point of view, how this book made me feel or what it made me think, great lines or quotes, etc.

Overall rating: ☆☆☆☆☆

BOOK TITLE:

Author:

Publisher:

Number of pages:

Fiction ☐ Genre:

Nonfiction ☐ Subject:

How I discovered or acquired this book:

When & where read:

Noteworthy experiences while reading this book:

Check out author's other books? ☐ Or related books? ☐
(If yes, add them to **Books I'd Like to Read**—see page 145.)

Rate on a scale of 1 to 10 (10 being exceptional):

Quality of writing	1	2	3	4	5	6	7	8	9	10	NA
Pace	1	2	3	4	5	6	7	8	9	10	NA
Plot development	1	2	3	4	5	6	7	8	9	10	NA
Characters	1	2	3	4	5	6	7	8	9	10	NA
Enjoyability	1	2	3	4	5	6	7	8	9	10	NA
Insightfulness	1	2	3	4	5	6	7	8	9	10	NA
Ease of reading	1	2	3	4	5	6	7	8	9	10	NA
Photos/Illustrations	1	2	3	4	5	6	7	8	9	10	NA

Recommend this book? ☐ To whom?

NOTES AND OPINIONS:
Basic plot or contents, setting, main characters, point of view, how this book made me feel or what it made me think, great lines or quotes, etc.

Overall rating: ☆☆☆☆☆

BOOK TITLE:

Author:

Publisher:

Number of pages:

Fiction ☐ Genre:

Nonfiction ☐ Subject:

How I discovered or acquired this book:

When & where read:

Noteworthy experiences while reading this book:

Check out author's other books? ☐ Or related books? ☐
(If yes, add them to **Books I'd Like to Read**—see page 145.)

Rate on a scale of 1 to 10 (10 being exceptional):

Quality of writing	1	2	3	4	5	6	7	8	9	10	NA
Pace	1	2	3	4	5	6	7	8	9	10	NA
Plot development	1	2	3	4	5	6	7	8	9	10	NA
Characters	1	2	3	4	5	6	7	8	9	10	NA
Enjoyability	1	2	3	4	5	6	7	8	9	10	NA
Insightfulness	1	2	3	4	5	6	7	8	9	10	NA
Ease of reading	1	2	3	4	5	6	7	8	9	10	NA
Photos/Illustrations	1	2	3	4	5	6	7	8	9	10	NA

Recommend this book? ☐ To whom?

NOTES AND OPINIONS:

Basic plot or contents, setting, main characters, point of view, how this book made me feel or what it made me think, great lines or quotes, etc.

Overall rating: ☆☆☆☆☆

BOOK TITLE:

Author:

Publisher:

Number of pages:

Fiction ☐ Genre:

Nonfiction ☐ Subject:

How I discovered or acquired this book:

When & where read:

Noteworthy experiences while reading this book:

Check out author's other books? ☐ Or related books? ☐
(If yes, add them to **Books I'd Like to Read**—see page 145.)

Rate on a scale of 1 to 10 (10 being exceptional):

Quality of writing	1	2	3	4	5	6	7	8	9	10	NA
Pace	1	2	3	4	5	6	7	8	9	10	NA
Plot development	1	2	3	4	5	6	7	8	9	10	NA
Characters	1	2	3	4	5	6	7	8	9	10	NA
Enjoyability	1	2	3	4	5	6	7	8	9	10	NA
Insightfulness	1	2	3	4	5	6	7	8	9	10	NA
Ease of reading	1	2	3	4	5	6	7	8	9	10	NA
Photos/Illustrations	1	2	3	4	5	6	7	8	9	10	NA

Recommend this book? ☐ To whom?

NOTES AND OPINIONS:
Basic plot or contents, setting, main characters, point of view, how this book made me feel or what it made me think, great lines or quotes, etc.

Overall rating: ☆☆☆☆☆

BOOK TITLE:

Author:

Publisher:

Number of pages:

Fiction ☐ Genre:

Nonfiction ☐ Subject:

How I discovered or acquired this book:

When & where read:

Noteworthy experiences while reading this book:

Check out author's other books? ☐ Or related books? ☐
(If yes, add them to **Books I'd Like to Read**—see page 145.)

Rate on a scale of 1 to 10 (10 being exceptional):

Quality of writing	1	2	3	4	5	6	7	8	9	10	NA
Pace	1	2	3	4	5	6	7	8	9	10	NA
Plot development	1	2	3	4	5	6	7	8	9	10	NA
Characters	1	2	3	4	5	6	7	8	9	10	NA
Enjoyability	1	2	3	4	5	6	7	8	9	10	NA
Insightfulness	1	2	3	4	5	6	7	8	9	10	NA
Ease of reading	1	2	3	4	5	6	7	8	9	10	NA
Photos/Illustrations	1	2	3	4	5	6	7	8	9	10	NA

Recommend this book? ☐ To whom?

NOTES AND OPINIONS:

Basic plot or contents, setting, main characters, point of view, how this book made me feel or what it made me think, great lines or quotes, etc.

Overall rating: ☆☆☆☆☆

BOOK TITLE:

Author:

Publisher:

Number of pages:

Fiction ☐ Genre:

Nonfiction ☐ Subject:

How I discovered or acquired this book:

When & where read:

Noteworthy experiences while reading this book:

Check out author's other books? ☐ Or related books? ☐
(If yes, add them to **Books I'd Like to Read**—see page 145.)

Rate on a scale of 1 to 10 (10 being exceptional):

Quality of writing	1	2	3	4	5	6	7	8	9	10	NA
Pace	1	2	3	4	5	6	7	8	9	10	NA
Plot development	1	2	3	4	5	6	7	8	9	10	NA
Characters	1	2	3	4	5	6	7	8	9	10	NA
Enjoyability	1	2	3	4	5	6	7	8	9	10	NA
Insightfulness	1	2	3	4	5	6	7	8	9	10	NA
Ease of reading	1	2	3	4	5	6	7	8	9	10	NA
Photos/Illustrations	1	2	3	4	5	6	7	8	9	10	NA

Recommend this book? ☐ To whom?

NOTES AND OPINIONS:

Basic plot or contents, setting, main characters, point of view, how this book made me feel or what it made me think, great lines or quotes, etc.

_____

_____

_____

_____

_____

_____

_____

_____

_____

_____

_____

_____

_____

_____

_____

_____

_____

_____

_____

_____

_____

_____

Overall rating: ☆☆☆☆☆

BOOK TITLE:

Author:

Publisher:

Number of pages:

Fiction ☐ Genre:

Nonfiction ☐ Subject:

How I discovered or acquired this book:

When & where read:

Noteworthy experiences while reading this book:

Check out author's other books? ☐ Or related books? ☐
(If yes, add them to **Books I'd Like to Read**—see page 145.)

Rate on a scale of 1 to 10 (10 being exceptional):

Quality of writing	1	2	3	4	5	6	7	8	9	10	NA
Pace	1	2	3	4	5	6	7	8	9	10	NA
Plot development	1	2	3	4	5	6	7	8	9	10	NA
Characters	1	2	3	4	5	6	7	8	9	10	NA
Enjoyability	1	2	3	4	5	6	7	8	9	10	NA
Insightfulness	1	2	3	4	5	6	7	8	9	10	NA
Ease of reading	1	2	3	4	5	6	7	8	9	10	NA
Photos/Illustrations	1	2	3	4	5	6	7	8	9	10	NA

Recommend this book? ☐ To whom?

NOTES AND OPINIONS:

Basic plot or contents, setting, main characters, point of view, how this book made me feel or what it made me think, great lines or quotes, etc.

Overall rating: ☆☆☆☆☆

BOOK TITLE:

Author:

Publisher:

Number of pages:

Fiction ☐ Genre:

Nonfiction ☐ Subject:

How I discovered or acquired this book:

When & where read:

Noteworthy experiences while reading this book:

Check out author's other books? ☐ Or related books? ☐
(If yes, add them to **Books I'd Like to Read**—see page 145.)

Rate on a scale of 1 to 10 (10 being exceptional):

Quality of writing	1	2	3	4	5	6	7	8	9	10	NA
Pace	1	2	3	4	5	6	7	8	9	10	NA
Plot development	1	2	3	4	5	6	7	8	9	10	NA
Characters	1	2	3	4	5	6	7	8	9	10	NA
Enjoyability	1	2	3	4	5	6	7	8	9	10	NA
Insightfulness	1	2	3	4	5	6	7	8	9	10	NA
Ease of reading	1	2	3	4	5	6	7	8	9	10	NA
Photos/Illustrations	1	2	3	4	5	6	7	8	9	10	NA

Recommend this book? ☐ To whom?

NOTES AND OPINIONS:

Basic plot or contents, setting, main characters, point of view, how this book made me feel or what it made me think, great lines or quotes, etc.

_____

_____

_____

_____

_____

_____

_____

_____

_____

_____

_____

_____

_____

_____

_____

_____

_____

_____

_____

_____

_____

_____

_____

Overall rating: ☆☆☆☆☆

BOOK TITLE:

Author:

Publisher:

Number of pages:

Fiction ☐ Genre:

Nonfiction ☐ Subject:

How I discovered or acquired this book:

When & where read:

Noteworthy experiences while reading this book:

Check out author's other books? ☐ Or related books? ☐
(If yes, add them to **Books I'd Like to Read**—see page 145.)

Rate on a scale of 1 to 10 (10 being exceptional):

Quality of writing	1	2	3	4	5	6	7	8	9	10	NA
Pace	1	2	3	4	5	6	7	8	9	10	NA
Plot development	1	2	3	4	5	6	7	8	9	10	NA
Characters	1	2	3	4	5	6	7	8	9	10	NA
Enjoyability	1	2	3	4	5	6	7	8	9	10	NA
Insightfulness	1	2	3	4	5	6	7	8	9	10	NA
Ease of reading	1	2	3	4	5	6	7	8	9	10	NA
Photos/Illustrations	1	2	3	4	5	6	7	8	9	10	NA

Recommend this book? ☐ To whom?

NOTES AND OPINIONS:

Basic plot or contents, setting, main characters, point of view, how this book made me feel or what it made me think, great lines or quotes, etc.

_____

_____

_____

_____

_____

_____

_____

_____

_____

_____

_____

_____

_____

_____

_____

_____

_____

_____

_____

_____

_____

_____

_____

_____

_____

Overall rating: ☆☆☆☆☆

BOOK TITLE:

Author:

Publisher:

Number of pages:

Fiction ☐ Genre:

Nonfiction ☐ Subject:

How I discovered or acquired this book:

When & where read:

Noteworthy experiences while reading this book:

Check out author's other books? ☐ Or related books? ☐
(If yes, add them to **Books I'd Like to Read**—see page 145.)

Rate on a scale of 1 to 10 (10 being exceptional):

Quality of writing	1	2	3	4	5	6	7	8	9	10	NA
Pace	1	2	3	4	5	6	7	8	9	10	NA
Plot development	1	2	3	4	5	6	7	8	9	10	NA
Characters	1	2	3	4	5	6	7	8	9	10	NA
Enjoyability	1	2	3	4	5	6	7	8	9	10	NA
Insightfulness	1	2	3	4	5	6	7	8	9	10	NA
Ease of reading	1	2	3	4	5	6	7	8	9	10	NA
Photos/Illustrations	1	2	3	4	5	6	7	8	9	10	NA

Recommend this book? ☐ To whom?

NOTES AND OPINIONS:
Basic plot or contents, setting, main characters, point of view, how this book made me feel or what it made me think, great lines or quotes, etc.

_____

_____

_____

_____

_____

_____

_____

_____

_____

_____

_____

_____

_____

_____

_____

_____

_____

_____

_____

_____

_____

_____

Overall rating: ☆☆☆☆☆

BOOK TITLE:

Author:

Publisher:

Number of pages:

Fiction ☐ Genre:

Nonfiction ☐ Subject:

How I discovered or acquired this book:

When & where read:

Noteworthy experiences while reading this book:

Check out author's other books? ☐ Or related books? ☐
(If yes, add them to **Books I'd Like to Read**—see page 145.)

Rate on a scale of 1 to 10 (10 being exceptional):

Quality of writing	1	2	3	4	5	6	7	8	9	10	NA
Pace	1	2	3	4	5	6	7	8	9	10	NA
Plot development	1	2	3	4	5	6	7	8	9	10	NA
Characters	1	2	3	4	5	6	7	8	9	10	NA
Enjoyability	1	2	3	4	5	6	7	8	9	10	NA
Insightfulness	1	2	3	4	5	6	7	8	9	10	NA
Ease of reading	1	2	3	4	5	6	7	8	9	10	NA
Photos/Illustrations	1	2	3	4	5	6	7	8	9	10	NA

Recommend this book? ☐ To whom?

NOTES AND OPINIONS:

Basic plot or contents, setting, main characters, point of view, how this book made me feel or what it made me think, great lines or quotes, etc.

Overall rating: ☆☆☆☆☆

BOOK TITLE:

Author:

Publisher:

Number of pages:

Fiction ☐ Genre:

Nonfiction ☐ Subject:

How I discovered or acquired this book:

When & where read:

Noteworthy experiences while reading this book:

Check out author's other books? ☐ Or related books? ☐
(If yes, add them to **Books I'd Like to Read**—see page 145.)

Rate on a scale of 1 to 10 (10 being exceptional):

Quality of writing	1	2	3	4	5	6	7	8	9	10	NA
Pace	1	2	3	4	5	6	7	8	9	10	NA
Plot development	1	2	3	4	5	6	7	8	9	10	NA
Characters	1	2	3	4	5	6	7	8	9	10	NA
Enjoyability	1	2	3	4	5	6	7	8	9	10	NA
Insightfulness	1	2	3	4	5	6	7	8	9	10	NA
Ease of reading	1	2	3	4	5	6	7	8	9	10	NA
Photos/Illustrations	1	2	3	4	5	6	7	8	9	10	NA

Recommend this book? ☐ To whom?

NOTES AND OPINIONS:

Basic plot or contents, setting, main characters, point of view, how this book made me feel or what it made me think, great lines or quotes, etc.

_____

_____

_____

_____

_____

_____

_____

_____

_____

_____

_____

_____

_____

_____

_____

_____

_____

_____

_____

_____

_____

_____

Overall rating: ☆☆☆☆☆

BOOK TITLE:

Author:

Publisher:

Number of pages:

Fiction ☐ Genre:

Nonfiction ☐ Subject:

How I discovered or acquired this book:

When & where read:

Noteworthy experiences while reading this book:

Check out author's other books? ☐ Or related books? ☐
(If yes, add them to **Books I'd Like to Read**—see page 145.)

Rate on a scale of 1 to 10 (10 being exceptional):

Quality of writing	1	2	3	4	5	6	7	8	9	10	NA
Pace	1	2	3	4	5	6	7	8	9	10	NA
Plot development	1	2	3	4	5	6	7	8	9	10	NA
Characters	1	2	3	4	5	6	7	8	9	10	NA
Enjoyability	1	2	3	4	5	6	7	8	9	10	NA
Insightfulness	1	2	3	4	5	6	7	8	9	10	NA
Ease of reading	1	2	3	4	5	6	7	8	9	10	NA
Photos/Illustrations	1	2	3	4	5	6	7	8	9	10	NA

Recommend this book? ☐ To whom?

NOTES AND OPINIONS:

Basic plot or contents, setting, main characters, point of view, how this book made me feel or what it made me think, great lines or quotes, etc.

....

....

....

....

....

....

....

....

....

....

....

....

....

....

....

....

....

....

....

Overall rating: ☆☆☆☆☆

BOOK TITLE:

Author:

Publisher:

Number of pages:

Fiction ☐ Genre:

Nonfiction ☐ Subject:

How I discovered or acquired this book:

When & where read:

Noteworthy experiences while reading this book:

Check out author's other books? ☐ Or related books? ☐
(If yes, add them to **Books I'd Like to Read**—see page 145.)

Rate on a scale of 1 to 10 (10 being exceptional):

Quality of writing	1	2	3	4	5	6	7	8	9	10	NA
Pace	1	2	3	4	5	6	7	8	9	10	NA
Plot development	1	2	3	4	5	6	7	8	9	10	NA
Characters	1	2	3	4	5	6	7	8	9	10	NA
Enjoyability	1	2	3	4	5	6	7	8	9	10	NA
Insightfulness	1	2	3	4	5	6	7	8	9	10	NA
Ease of reading	1	2	3	4	5	6	7	8	9	10	NA
Photos/Illustrations	1	2	3	4	5	6	7	8	9	10	NA

Recommend this book? ☐ To whom?

NOTES AND OPINIONS:

Basic plot or contents, setting, main characters, point of view, how this book made me feel or what it made me think, great lines or quotes, etc.

_____

_____

_____

_____

_____

_____

_____

_____

_____

_____

_____

_____

_____

_____

_____

_____

_____

_____

_____

_____

_____

_____

_____

_____

_____

Overall rating: ☆☆☆☆☆

BOOK TITLE:

Author:

Publisher:

Number of pages:

Fiction ☐ Genre:

Nonfiction ☐ Subject:

How I discovered or acquired this book:

When & where read:

Noteworthy experiences while reading this book:

Check out author's other books? ☐ Or related books? ☐
(If yes, add them to **Books I'd Like to Read**—see page 145.)

Rate on a scale of 1 to 10 (10 being exceptional):

Quality of writing	1	2	3	4	5	6	7	8	9	10	NA
Pace	1	2	3	4	5	6	7	8	9	10	NA
Plot development	1	2	3	4	5	6	7	8	9	10	NA
Characters	1	2	3	4	5	6	7	8	9	10	NA
Enjoyability	1	2	3	4	5	6	7	8	9	10	NA
Insightfulness	1	2	3	4	5	6	7	8	9	10	NA
Ease of reading	1	2	3	4	5	6	7	8	9	10	NA
Photos/Illustrations	1	2	3	4	5	6	7	8	9	10	NA

Recommend this book? ☐ To whom?

NOTES AND OPINIONS:
Basic plot or contents, setting, main characters, point of view, how this book made me feel or what it made me think, great lines or quotes, etc.

_____

_____

_____

_____

_____

_____

_____

_____

_____

_____

_____

_____

_____

_____

_____

_____

_____

_____

_____

_____

Overall rating: ☆☆☆☆☆

BOOK TITLE:

Author:

Publisher:

Number of pages:

Fiction ☐ Genre:

Nonfiction ☐ Subject:

How I discovered or acquired this book:

When & where read:

Noteworthy experiences while reading this book:

Check out author's other books? ☐ Or related books? ☐
(If yes, add them to **Books I'd Like to Read**—see page 145.)

Rate on a scale of 1 to 10 (10 being exceptional):

Quality of writing	1	2	3	4	5	6	7	8	9	10	NA
Pace	1	2	3	4	5	6	7	8	9	10	NA
Plot development	1	2	3	4	5	6	7	8	9	10	NA
Characters	1	2	3	4	5	6	7	8	9	10	NA
Enjoyability	1	2	3	4	5	6	7	8	9	10	NA
Insightfulness	1	2	3	4	5	6	7	8	9	10	NA
Ease of reading	1	2	3	4	5	6	7	8	9	10	NA
Photos/Illustrations	1	2	3	4	5	6	7	8	9	10	NA

Recommend this book? ☐ To whom?

NOTES AND OPINIONS:

Basic plot or contents, setting, main characters, point of view, how this book made me feel or what it made me think, great lines or quotes, etc.

_____

_____

_____

_____

_____

_____

_____

_____

_____

_____

_____

_____

_____

_____

_____

_____

_____

_____

_____

_____

_____

_____

_____

_____

Overall rating: ☆☆☆☆☆

BOOK TITLE:

Author:

Publisher:

Number of pages:

Fiction ☐ Genre:

Nonfiction ☐ Subject:

How I discovered or acquired this book:

When & where read:

Noteworthy experiences while reading this book:

Check out author's other books? ☐ Or related books? ☐
(If yes, add them to **Books I'd Like to Read**—see page 145.)

Rate on a scale of 1 to 10 (10 being exceptional):

Quality of writing	1	2	3	4	5	6	7	8	9	10	NA
Pace	1	2	3	4	5	6	7	8	9	10	NA
Plot development	1	2	3	4	5	6	7	8	9	10	NA
Characters	1	2	3	4	5	6	7	8	9	10	NA
Enjoyability	1	2	3	4	5	6	7	8	9	10	NA
Insightfulness	1	2	3	4	5	6	7	8	9	10	NA
Ease of reading	1	2	3	4	5	6	7	8	9	10	NA
Photos/Illustrations	1	2	3	4	5	6	7	8	9	10	NA

Recommend this book? ☐ To whom?

NOTES AND OPINIONS:

Basic plot or contents, setting, main characters, point of view, how this book made me feel or what it made me think, great lines or quotes, etc.

Overall rating: ☆☆☆☆☆

BOOK TITLE:

Author:

Publisher:

Number of pages:

Fiction ☐ Genre:

Nonfiction ☐ Subject:

How I discovered or acquired this book:

When & where read:

Noteworthy experiences while reading this book:

Check out author's other books? ☐ Or related books? ☐
(If yes, add them to **Books I'd Like to Read**—see page 145.)

Rate on a scale of 1 to 10 (10 being exceptional):

Quality of writing	1	2	3	4	5	6	7	8	9	10	NA
Pace	1	2	3	4	5	6	7	8	9	10	NA
Plot development	1	2	3	4	5	6	7	8	9	10	NA
Characters	1	2	3	4	5	6	7	8	9	10	NA
Enjoyability	1	2	3	4	5	6	7	8	9	10	NA
Insightfulness	1	2	3	4	5	6	7	8	9	10	NA
Ease of reading	1	2	3	4	5	6	7	8	9	10	NA
Photos/Illustrations	1	2	3	4	5	6	7	8	9	10	NA

Recommend this book? ☐ To whom?

NOTES AND OPINIONS:

Basic plot or contents, setting, main characters, point of view, how this book made me feel or what it made me think, great lines or quotes, etc.

Overall rating: ☆☆☆☆☆

BOOK TITLE:

Author:

Publisher:

Number of pages:

Fiction ☐ Genre:

Nonfiction ☐ Subject:

How I discovered or acquired this book:

When & where read:

Noteworthy experiences while reading this book:

Check out author's other books? ☐ Or related books? ☐
(If yes, add them to **Books I'd Like to Read**—see page 145.)

Rate on a scale of 1 to 10 (10 being exceptional):

Quality of writing	1	2	3	4	5	6	7	8	9	10	NA
Pace	1	2	3	4	5	6	7	8	9	10	NA
Plot development	1	2	3	4	5	6	7	8	9	10	NA
Characters	1	2	3	4	5	6	7	8	9	10	NA
Enjoyability	1	2	3	4	5	6	7	8	9	10	NA
Insightfulness	1	2	3	4	5	6	7	8	9	10	NA
Ease of reading	1	2	3	4	5	6	7	8	9	10	NA
Photos/Illustrations	1	2	3	4	5	6	7	8	9	10	NA

Recommend this book? ☐ To whom?

NOTES AND OPINIONS:

Basic plot or contents, setting, main characters, point of view, how this book made me feel or what it made me think, great lines or quotes, etc.

_____

_____

_____

_____

_____

_____

_____

_____

_____

_____

_____

_____

_____

_____

_____

_____

_____

_____

_____

_____

Overall rating: ☆☆☆☆☆

BOOK TITLE:

Author:

Publisher:

Number of pages:

Fiction ☐ Genre:

Nonfiction ☐ Subject:

How I discovered or acquired this book:

When & where read:

Noteworthy experiences while reading this book:

Check out author's other books? ☐ Or related books? ☐
(If yes, add them to **Books I'd Like to Read**—see page 145.)

Rate on a scale of 1 to 10 (10 being exceptional):

Quality of writing	1	2	3	4	5	6	7	8	9	10	NA
Pace	1	2	3	4	5	6	7	8	9	10	NA
Plot development	1	2	3	4	5	6	7	8	9	10	NA
Characters	1	2	3	4	5	6	7	8	9	10	NA
Enjoyability	1	2	3	4	5	6	7	8	9	10	NA
Insightfulness	1	2	3	4	5	6	7	8	9	10	NA
Ease of reading	1	2	3	4	5	6	7	8	9	10	NA
Photos/Illustrations	1	2	3	4	5	6	7	8	9	10	NA

Recommend this book? ☐ To whom?

NOTES AND OPINIONS:

Basic plot or contents, setting, main characters, point of view, how this book made me feel or what it made me think, great lines or quotes, etc.

Overall rating: ☆☆☆☆☆

BOOK TITLE:

Author:

Publisher:

Number of pages:

Fiction ☐ Genre:

Nonfiction ☐ Subject:

How I discovered or acquired this book:

When & where read:

Noteworthy experiences while reading this book:

Check out author's other books? ☐ Or related books? ☐
(If yes, add them to **Books I'd Like to Read**—see page 145.)

Rate on a scale of 1 to 10 (10 being exceptional):

Quality of writing	1	2	3	4	5	6	7	8	9	10	NA
Pace	1	2	3	4	5	6	7	8	9	10	NA
Plot development	1	2	3	4	5	6	7	8	9	10	NA
Characters	1	2	3	4	5	6	7	8	9	10	NA
Enjoyability	1	2	3	4	5	6	7	8	9	10	NA
Insightfulness	1	2	3	4	5	6	7	8	9	10	NA
Ease of reading	1	2	3	4	5	6	7	8	9	10	NA
Photos/Illustrations	1	2	3	4	5	6	7	8	9	10	NA

Recommend this book? ☐ To whom?

NOTES AND OPINIONS:
Basic plot or contents, setting, main characters, point of view, how this
book made me feel or what it made me think, great lines or quotes, etc.

....

....

....

....

....

....

....

....

....

....

....

....

....

....

....

....

....

....

....

....

....

Overall rating: ☆☆☆☆☆

BOOK TITLE:

Author:

Publisher:

Number of pages:

Fiction ☐ Genre:

Nonfiction ☐ Subject:

How I discovered or acquired this book:

When & where read:

Noteworthy experiences while reading this book:

Check out author's other books? ☐ Or related books? ☐
(If yes, add them to **Books I'd Like to Read**—see page 145.)

Rate on a scale of 1 to 10 (10 being exceptional):

Quality of writing	1	2	3	4	5	6	7	8	9	10	NA
Pace	1	2	3	4	5	6	7	8	9	10	NA
Plot development	1	2	3	4	5	6	7	8	9	10	NA
Characters	1	2	3	4	5	6	7	8	9	10	NA
Enjoyability	1	2	3	4	5	6	7	8	9	10	NA
Insightfulness	1	2	3	4	5	6	7	8	9	10	NA
Ease of reading	1	2	3	4	5	6	7	8	9	10	NA
Photos/Illustrations	1	2	3	4	5	6	7	8	9	10	NA

Recommend this book? ☐ To whom?

NOTES AND OPINIONS:

Basic plot or contents, setting, main characters, point of view, how this book made me feel or what it made me think, great lines or quotes, etc.

_____
_____
_____
_____
_____
_____
_____
_____
_____
_____
_____
_____
_____
_____
_____
_____
_____
_____
_____
_____
_____

Overall rating: ☆☆☆☆☆

BOOK TITLE:

Author:

Publisher:

Number of pages:

Fiction ☐ Genre:

Nonfiction ☐ Subject:

How I discovered or acquired this book:

When & where read:

Noteworthy experiences while reading this book:

Check out author's other books? ☐ Or related books? ☐
(If yes, add them to **Books I'd Like to Read**—see page 145.)

Rate on a scale of 1 to 10 (10 being exceptional):

Quality of writing	1	2	3	4	5	6	7	8	9	10	NA
Pace	1	2	3	4	5	6	7	8	9	10	NA
Plot development	1	2	3	4	5	6	7	8	9	10	NA
Characters	1	2	3	4	5	6	7	8	9	10	NA
Enjoyability	1	2	3	4	5	6	7	8	9	10	NA
Insightfulness	1	2	3	4	5	6	7	8	9	10	NA
Ease of reading	1	2	3	4	5	6	7	8	9	10	NA
Photos/Illustrations	1	2	3	4	5	6	7	8	9	10	NA

Recommend this book? ☐ To whom?

NOTES AND OPINIONS:

Basic plot or contents, setting, main characters, point of view, how this book made me feel or what it made me think, great lines or quotes, etc.

Overall rating: ☆☆☆☆☆

BOOK TITLE:

Author:

Publisher:

Number of pages:

Fiction ☐ Genre:

Nonfiction ☐ Subject:

How I discovered or acquired this book:

When & where read:

Noteworthy experiences while reading this book:

Check out author's other books? ☐ Or related books? ☐
(If yes, add them to **Books I'd Like to Read**—see page 145.)

Rate on a scale of 1 to 10 (10 being exceptional):

Quality of writing	1	2	3	4	5	6	7	8	9	10	NA
Pace	1	2	3	4	5	6	7	8	9	10	NA
Plot development	1	2	3	4	5	6	7	8	9	10	NA
Characters	1	2	3	4	5	6	7	8	9	10	NA
Enjoyability	1	2	3	4	5	6	7	8	9	10	NA
Insightfulness	1	2	3	4	5	6	7	8	9	10	NA
Ease of reading	1	2	3	4	5	6	7	8	9	10	NA
Photos/Illustrations	1	2	3	4	5	6	7	8	9	10	NA

Recommend this book? ☐ To whom?

NOTES AND OPINIONS:

Basic plot or contents, setting, main characters, point of view, how this book made me feel or what it made me think, great lines or quotes, etc.

Overall rating: ☆☆☆☆☆

BOOK TITLE:

Author:

Publisher:

Number of pages:

Fiction ☐ Genre:

Nonfiction ☐ Subject:

How I discovered or acquired this book:

When & where read:

Noteworthy experiences while reading this book:

Check out author's other books? ☐ Or related books? ☐
(If yes, add them to **Books I'd Like to Read**—see page 145.)

Rate on a scale of 1 to 10 (10 being exceptional):

	1	2	3	4	5	6	7	8	9	10	NA
Quality of writing	1	2	3	4	5	6	7	8	9	10	NA
Pace	1	2	3	4	5	6	7	8	9	10	NA
Plot development	1	2	3	4	5	6	7	8	9	10	NA
Characters	1	2	3	4	5	6	7	8	9	10	NA
Enjoyability	1	2	3	4	5	6	7	8	9	10	NA
Insightfulness	1	2	3	4	5	6	7	8	9	10	NA
Ease of reading	1	2	3	4	5	6	7	8	9	10	NA
Photos/Illustrations	1	2	3	4	5	6	7	8	9	10	NA

Recommend this book? ☐ To whom?

NOTES AND OPINIONS:

Basic plot or contents, setting, main characters, point of view, how this book made me feel or what it made me think, great lines or quotes, etc.

Overall rating: ☆☆☆☆☆

BOOK TITLE:

Author:

Publisher:

Number of pages:

Fiction ☐ Genre:

Nonfiction ☐ Subject:

How I discovered or acquired this book:

When & where read:

Noteworthy experiences while reading this book:

Check out author's other books? ☐ Or related books? ☐
(If yes, add them to **Books I'd Like to Read**—see page 145.)

Rate on a scale of 1 to 10 (10 being exceptional):

Quality of writing	1 2 3 4 5 6 7 8 9 10 NA
Pace	1 2 3 4 5 6 7 8 9 10 NA
Plot development	1 2 3 4 5 6 7 8 9 10 NA
Characters	1 2 3 4 5 6 7 8 9 10 NA
Enjoyability	1 2 3 4 5 6 7 8 9 10 NA
Insightfulness	1 2 3 4 5 6 7 8 9 10 NA
Ease of reading	1 2 3 4 5 6 7 8 9 10 NA
Photos/Illustrations	1 2 3 4 5 6 7 8 9 10 NA

Recommend this book? ☐ To whom?

NOTES AND OPINIONS:

Basic plot or contents, setting, main characters, point of view, how this book made me feel or what it made me think, great lines or quotes, etc.

Overall rating: ☆☆☆☆☆

BOOK TITLE:

Author:

Publisher:

Number of pages:

Fiction ☐ Genre:

Nonfiction ☐ Subject:

How I discovered or acquired this book:

When & where read:

Noteworthy experiences while reading this book:

Check out author's other books? ☐ Or related books? ☐
(If yes, add them to **Books I'd Like to Read**—see page 145.)

Rate on a scale of 1 to 10 (10 being exceptional):

Quality of writing	1	2	3	4	5	6	7	8	9	10	NA
Pace	1	2	3	4	5	6	7	8	9	10	NA
Plot development	1	2	3	4	5	6	7	8	9	10	NA
Characters	1	2	3	4	5	6	7	8	9	10	NA
Enjoyability	1	2	3	4	5	6	7	8	9	10	NA
Insightfulness	1	2	3	4	5	6	7	8	9	10	NA
Ease of reading	1	2	3	4	5	6	7	8	9	10	NA
Photos/Illustrations	1	2	3	4	5	6	7	8	9	10	NA

Recommend this book? ☐ To whom?

NOTES AND OPINIONS:

Basic plot or contents, setting, main characters, point of view, how this book made me feel or what it made me think, great lines or quotes, etc.

Overall rating: ☆☆☆☆☆

BOOK TITLE:

Author:

Publisher:

Number of pages:

Fiction ☐ Genre:

Nonfiction ☐ Subject:

How I discovered or acquired this book:

When & where read:

Noteworthy experiences while reading this book:

Check out author's other books? ☐ Or related books? ☐
(If yes, add them to **Books I'd Like to Read**—see page 145.)

Rate on a scale of 1 to 10 (10 being exceptional):

Quality of writing	1	2	3	4	5	6	7	8	9	10	NA
Pace	1	2	3	4	5	6	7	8	9	10	NA
Plot development	1	2	3	4	5	6	7	8	9	10	NA
Characters	1	2	3	4	5	6	7	8	9	10	NA
Enjoyability	1	2	3	4	5	6	7	8	9	10	NA
Insightfulness	1	2	3	4	5	6	7	8	9	10	NA
Ease of reading	1	2	3	4	5	6	7	8	9	10	NA
Photos/Illustrations	1	2	3	4	5	6	7	8	9	10	NA

Recommend this book? ☐ To whom?

NOTES AND OPINIONS:

Basic plot or contents, setting, main characters, point of view, how this book made me feel or what it made me think, great lines or quotes, etc.

Overall rating: ☆☆☆☆☆

BOOK TITLE:

Author:

Publisher:

Number of pages:

Fiction ☐ Genre:

Nonfiction ☐ Subject:

How I discovered or acquired this book:

When & where read:

Noteworthy experiences while reading this book:

Check out author's other books? ☐ Or related books? ☐
(If yes, add them to **Books I'd Like to Read**—see page 145.)

Rate on a scale of 1 to 10 (10 being exceptional):

Quality of writing	1	2	3	4	5	6	7	8	9	10	NA
Pace	1	2	3	4	5	6	7	8	9	10	NA
Plot development	1	2	3	4	5	6	7	8	9	10	NA
Characters	1	2	3	4	5	6	7	8	9	10	NA
Enjoyability	1	2	3	4	5	6	7	8	9	10	NA
Insightfulness	1	2	3	4	5	6	7	8	9	10	NA
Ease of reading	1	2	3	4	5	6	7	8	9	10	NA
Photos/Illustrations	1	2	3	4	5	6	7	8	9	10	NA

Recommend this book? ☐ To whom?

NOTES AND OPINIONS:

Basic plot or contents, setting, main characters, point of view, how this book made me feel or what it made me think, great lines or quotes, etc.

Overall rating: ☆☆☆☆☆

BOOK TITLE:

Author:

Publisher:

Number of pages:

Fiction ☐ Genre:

Nonfiction ☐ Subject:

How I discovered or acquired this book:

When & where read:

Noteworthy experiences while reading this book:

Check out author's other books? ☐ Or related books? ☐
(If yes, add them to **Books I'd Like to Read**—see page 145.)

Rate on a scale of 1 to 10 (10 being exceptional):

Quality of writing	1	2	3	4	5	6	7	8	9	10	NA
Pace	1	2	3	4	5	6	7	8	9	10	NA
Plot development	1	2	3	4	5	6	7	8	9	10	NA
Characters	1	2	3	4	5	6	7	8	9	10	NA
Enjoyability	1	2	3	4	5	6	7	8	9	10	NA
Insightfulness	1	2	3	4	5	6	7	8	9	10	NA
Ease of reading	1	2	3	4	5	6	7	8	9	10	NA
Photos/Illustrations	1	2	3	4	5	6	7	8	9	10	NA

Recommend this book? ☐ To whom?

NOTES AND OPINIONS:

Basic plot or contents, setting, main characters, point of view, how this book made me feel or what it made me think, great lines or quotes, etc.

Overall rating: ☆☆☆☆☆

BOOK TITLE:

Author:

Publisher:

Number of pages:

Fiction ☐ Genre:

Nonfiction ☐ Subject:

How I discovered or acquired this book:

When & where read:

Noteworthy experiences while reading this book:

Check out author's other books? ☐ Or related books? ☐
(If yes, add them to **Books I'd Like to Read**—see page 145.)

Rate on a scale of 1 to 10 (10 being exceptional):

Quality of writing	1	2	3	4	5	6	7	8	9	10	NA
Pace	1	2	3	4	5	6	7	8	9	10	NA
Plot development	1	2	3	4	5	6	7	8	9	10	NA
Characters	1	2	3	4	5	6	7	8	9	10	NA
Enjoyability	1	2	3	4	5	6	7	8	9	10	NA
Insightfulness	1	2	3	4	5	6	7	8	9	10	NA
Ease of reading	1	2	3	4	5	6	7	8	9	10	NA
Photos/Illustrations	1	2	3	4	5	6	7	8	9	10	NA

Recommend this book? ☐ To whom?

NOTES AND OPINIONS:

Basic plot or contents, setting, main characters, point of view, how this
book made me feel or what it made me think, great lines or quotes, etc.

Overall rating: ☆☆☆☆☆

BOOK TITLE:

Author:

Publisher:

Number of pages:

Fiction ☐ Genre:

Nonfiction ☐ Subject:

How I discovered or acquired this book:

When & where read:

Noteworthy experiences while reading this book:

Check out author's other books? ☐ Or related books? ☐
(If yes, add them to **Books I'd Like to Read**—see page 145.)

Rate on a scale of 1 to 10 (10 being exceptional):

Quality of writing	1	2	3	4	5	6	7	8	9	10	NA
Pace	1	2	3	4	5	6	7	8	9	10	NA
Plot development	1	2	3	4	5	6	7	8	9	10	NA
Characters	1	2	3	4	5	6	7	8	9	10	NA
Enjoyability	1	2	3	4	5	6	7	8	9	10	NA
Insightfulness	1	2	3	4	5	6	7	8	9	10	NA
Ease of reading	1	2	3	4	5	6	7	8	9	10	NA
Photos/Illustrations	1	2	3	4	5	6	7	8	9	10	NA

Recommend this book? ☐ To whom?

NOTES AND OPINIONS:

Basic plot or contents, setting, main characters, point of view, how this
book made me feel or what it made me think, great lines or quotes, etc.

Overall rating: ☆☆☆☆☆

BOOK TITLE:

Author:

Publisher:

Number of pages:

Fiction ☐ Genre:

Nonfiction ☐ Subject:

How I discovered or acquired this book:

When & where read:

Noteworthy experiences while reading this book:

Check out author's other books? ☐ Or related books? ☐
(If yes, add them to **Books I'd Like to Read**—see page 145.)

Rate on a scale of 1 to 10 (10 being exceptional):

Quality of writing	1	2	3	4	5	6	7	8	9	10	NA
Pace	1	2	3	4	5	6	7	8	9	10	NA
Plot development	1	2	3	4	5	6	7	8	9	10	NA
Characters	1	2	3	4	5	6	7	8	9	10	NA
Enjoyability	1	2	3	4	5	6	7	8	9	10	NA
Insightfulness	1	2	3	4	5	6	7	8	9	10	NA
Ease of reading	1	2	3	4	5	6	7	8	9	10	NA
Photos/Illustrations	1	2	3	4	5	6	7	8	9	10	NA

Recommend this book? ☐ To whom?

NOTES AND OPINIONS:

Basic plot or contents, setting, main characters, point of view, how this book made me feel or what it made me think, great lines or quotes, etc.

_____

_____

_____

_____

_____

_____

_____

_____

_____

_____

_____

_____

_____

_____

_____

_____

_____

_____

_____

_____

Overall rating: ☆☆☆☆☆

BOOK TITLE:

Author:

Publisher:

Number of pages:

Fiction ☐ Genre:

Nonfiction ☐ Subject:

How I discovered or acquired this book:

When & where read:

Noteworthy experiences while reading this book:

Check out author's other books? ☐ Or related books? ☐
(If yes, add them to **Books I'd Like to Read**—see page 145.)

Rate on a scale of 1 to 10 (10 being exceptional):

Quality of writing	1	2	3	4	5	6	7	8	9	10	NA
Pace	1	2	3	4	5	6	7	8	9	10	NA
Plot development	1	2	3	4	5	6	7	8	9	10	NA
Characters	1	2	3	4	5	6	7	8	9	10	NA
Enjoyability	1	2	3	4	5	6	7	8	9	10	NA
Insightfulness	1	2	3	4	5	6	7	8	9	10	NA
Ease of reading	1	2	3	4	5	6	7	8	9	10	NA
Photos/Illustrations	1	2	3	4	5	6	7	8	9	10	NA

Recommend this book? ☐ To whom?

NOTES AND OPINIONS:

Basic plot or contents, setting, main characters, point of view, how this book made me feel or what it made me think, great lines or quotes, etc.

Overall rating: ☆☆☆☆☆

BOOK TITLE:

Author:

Publisher:

Number of pages:

Fiction ☐ Genre:

Nonfiction ☐ Subject:

How I discovered or acquired this book:

When & where read:

Noteworthy experiences while reading this book:

Check out author's other books? ☐ Or related books? ☐
(If yes, add them to **Books I'd Like to Read**—see page 145.)

Rate on a scale of 1 to 10 (10 being exceptional):

Quality of writing	1	2	3	4	5	6	7	8	9	10	NA
Pace	1	2	3	4	5	6	7	8	9	10	NA
Plot development	1	2	3	4	5	6	7	8	9	10	NA
Characters	1	2	3	4	5	6	7	8	9	10	NA
Enjoyability	1	2	3	4	5	6	7	8	9	10	NA
Insightfulness	1	2	3	4	5	6	7	8	9	10	NA
Ease of reading	1	2	3	4	5	6	7	8	9	10	NA
Photos/Illustrations	1	2	3	4	5	6	7	8	9	10	NA

Recommend this book? ☐ To whom?

NOTES AND OPINIONS:

Basic plot or contents, setting, main characters, point of view, how this book made me feel or what it made me think, great lines or quotes, etc.

Overall rating: ☆☆☆☆☆

*Where do I find the time
for not reading so many books?*

KARL KRAUS

BOOKS I'D LIKE TO READ
My reading wish list

Here is where you can keep a list of books you want to read. You know, the books friends recommend, forthcoming books from your favorite authors, or books in the news.

Use the next two pages (pages 146 and 147) as your own "Table of Contents" for your wish list. Write down the book title and the page on which your wish list entry for that title occurs. This will enable you to locate the information you need (exact title, author, etc.) when it's time at last to get your hands on that specific book.

Books I'd Like to Read *Table of Contents*

TITLE   Journal page number

BOOK TITLE

Author

Approximate length

Recommended by

Genre/subject

• •

BOOK TITLE

Author

Approximate length

Recommended by

Genre/subject

• •

BOOK TITLE

Author

Approximate length

Recommended by

Genre/subject

BOOK TITLE

Author

Approximate length

Recommended by

Genre/subject

∙∙∙

BOOK TITLE

Author

Approximate length

Recommended by

Genre/subject

∙∙∙

BOOK TITLE

Author

Approximate length

Recommended by

Genre/subject

BOOK TITLE

Author

Approximate length

Recommended by

Genre/subject

. . . .

BOOK TITLE

Author

Approximate length

Recommended by

Genre/subject

. . . .

BOOK TITLE

Author

Approximate length

Recommended by

Genre/subject

BOOK TITLE

Author

Approximate length

Recommended by

Genre/subject

. . . .

BOOK TITLE

Author

Approximate length

Recommended by

Genre/subject

. . . .

BOOK TITLE

Author

Approximate length

Recommended by

Genre/subject

BOOK TITLE

Author

Approximate length

Recommended by

Genre/subject

. . . .

BOOK TITLE

Author

Approximate length

Recommended by

Genre/subject

. . . .

BOOK TITLE

Author

Approximate length

Recommended by

Genre/subject

BOOK TITLE

Author

Approximate length

Recommended by

Genre/subject

• •

BOOK TITLE

Author

Approximate length

Recommended by

Genre/subject

• •

BOOK TITLE

Author

Approximate length

Recommended by

Genre/subject

BOOK TITLE

Author

Approximate length

Recommended by

Genre/subject

. . . .

BOOK TITLE

Author

Approximate length

Recommended by

Genre/subject

. . . .

BOOK TITLE

Author

Approximate length

Recommended by

Genre/subject

BOOK TITLE

Author

Approximate length

Recommended by

Genre/subject

. . . .

BOOK TITLE

Author

Approximate length

Recommended by

Genre/subject

. . . .

BOOK TITLE

Author

Approximate length

Recommended by

Genre/subject

BOOK TITLE

Author

Approximate length

Recommended by

Genre/subject

• •

BOOK TITLE

Author

Approximate length

Recommended by

Genre/subject

• •

BOOK TITLE

Author

Approximate length

Recommended by

Genre/subject

BOOK TITLE

Author

Approximate length

Recommended by

Genre/subject

. . . .

BOOK TITLE

Author

Approximate length

Recommended by

Genre/subject

. . . .

BOOK TITLE

Author

Approximate length

Recommended by

Genre/subject

BOOK TITLE

Author

Approximate length

Recommended by

Genre/subject

• •

BOOK TITLE

Author

Approximate length

Recommended by

Genre/subject

• •

BOOK TITLE

Author

Approximate length

Recommended by

Genre/subject

BOOK TITLE

Author

Approximate length

Recommended by

Genre/subject

• •

BOOK TITLE

Author

Approximate length

Recommended by

Genre/subject

• •

BOOK TITLE

Author

Approximate length

Recommended by

Genre/subject

BOOK TITLE

Author

Approximate length
Recommended by

Genre/subject

• •

BOOK TITLE

Author

Approximate length
Recommended by

Genre/subject

• •

BOOK TITLE

Author

Approximate length
Recommended by

Genre/subject

BOOK TITLE

Author

Approximate length

Recommended by

Genre/subject

· ·

BOOK TITLE

Author

Approximate length

Recommended by

Genre/subject

· ·

BOOK TITLE

Author

Approximate length

Recommended by

Genre/subject

BOOK TITLE

Author

Approximate length

Recommended by

Genre/subject

· ·

BOOK TITLE

Author

Approximate length

Recommended by

Genre/subject

· ·

BOOK TITLE

Author

Approximate length

Recommended by

Genre/subject

BOOK TITLE

Author

Approximate length

Recommended by

Genre/subject

· ·

BOOK TITLE

Author

Approximate length

Recommended by

Genre/subject

· ·

BOOK TITLE

Author

Approximate length

Recommended by

Genre/subject

BOOK TITLE

Author

Approximate length

Recommended by

Genre/subject

∙∙

BOOK TITLE

Author

Approximate length

Recommended by

Genre/subject

∙∙

BOOK TITLE

Author

Approximate length

Recommended by

Genre/subject

BOOK TITLE

Author

Approximate length

Recommended by

Genre/subject

. . . .

BOOK TITLE

Author

Approximate length

Recommended by

Genre/subject

. . . .

BOOK TITLE

Author

Approximate length

Recommended by

Genre/subject

BOOK TITLE

Author

Approximate length

Recommended by

Genre/subject

. . . .

BOOK TITLE

Author

Approximate length

Recommended by

Genre/subject

. . . .

BOOK TITLE

Author

Approximate length

Recommended by

Genre/subject

BOOK TITLE

Author

Approximate length

Recommended by

Genre/subject

· ·

BOOK TITLE

Author

Approximate length

Recommended by

Genre/subject

· ·

BOOK TITLE

Author

Approximate length

Recommended by

Genre/subject

Never lend books, for no one ever returns them; the only books I have in my library are books that other folks have lent to me.

ANATOLE FRANCE

MY BOOKS
Books bought, borrowed, lent, and given

Keep your book source contact information in this section, so it's handy when you want to order or reserve a book from your favorite bookseller or when borrowing books from the library. There are also pages for you to keep track of books you've borrowed, as well as space to record books you've lent to friends and family. We've even provided a place to write down books you've given and to whom, and books you want to give, and to whom.

OLD
RARE
NEW

Where I Get My Books
Bookstores, libraries, and other sources

*Where is human nature
so weak as in the bookstore?*

HENRY WARD BEECHER

NAME

Phone

Web site

User name

Password

Account number

· ·

NAME

Phone

Web site

User name

Password

Account number

· ·

NAME

Phone

Web site

User name

Password

Account number

NAME

Phone

Web site

User name

Password

Account number

••

NAME

Phone

Web site

User name

Password

Account number

••

NAME

Phone

Web site

User name

Password

Account number

••

NAME

Phone

Web site

User name

Password

Account number

NAME

Phone

Web site

User name

Password

Account number

. . . .

NAME

Phone

Web site

User name

Password

Account number

. . . .

NAME

Phone

Web site

User name

Password

Account number

. . . .

NAME

Phone

Web site

User name

Password

Account number

NAME

Phone

Web site

User name

Password

Account number

• •

NAME

Phone

Web site

User name

Password

Account number

• •

NAME

Phone

Web site

User name

Password

Account number

I have always imagined that
Paradise will be a kind of library.

JORGE LUIS BORGES

Books I've Borrowed

TITLE

Belongs to	When borrowed	When returned

Books I've Borrowed

TITLE

Belongs to	When borrowed	When returned

Books I've Lent

TITLE

Lent to	When lent	When returned

Books I've Lent

TITLE

Lent to	When lent	When returned

Books I've Given

TITLE   Given to

Books I Want to Give

TITLE   **To whom**

A great book should leave you with many experiences, and slightly exhausted at the end. You live several lives while reading.

WILLIAM STYRON

BOOK GROUP INFO
Friends and fellow readers

Keep up with your reading friends by using this section to record their contact information. You'll also find space for listing book group selections, and for your notes on meetings, locations, and related information.

Book Group Reading List

TITLE   Discussion date

Notes

Meeting locations and other information

Contacts

NAME

Contact info

Notes

....

NAME

Contact info

Notes

....

NAME

Contact info

Notes

....

NAME

Contact info

Notes

....

NAME

Contact info

Notes

••

NAME

Contact info

Notes

••

NAME

Contact info

Notes

••

NAME

Contact info

Notes

••

NAME

Contact info

Notes

••

NAME

Contact info

Notes

••

NAME

Contact info

Notes

••

NAME

Contact info

Notes

••

NAME

Contact info

Notes

• •

NAME

Contact info

Notes

• •

NAME

Contact info

Notes

• •

NAME

Contact info

Notes

• •

What really knocks me out is a book that, when you're all done reading it, you wish the author that wrote it was a terrific friend of yours and you could call him up on the phone whenever you felt like it.

J. D. SALINGER,
The Catcher in the Rye

ACCLAIMED AUTHORS AND BOOKS

Inspiration for future reading

Here you'll find several lists of award-winning authors and great books to inspire your future reading.

Recent Nobel Laureates in Literature

Most Nobel Prizes in Literature are awarded to writers for their career as a whole, not for specific titles. Here are thirty Literature Laureates to discover. For more information on the Nobel Prize in Literature, visit http://nobelprize.org/nobel_prizes/literature/

Svetlana Alexievich

Patrick Modiano

Alice Munro

Mo Yan

Tomas Tranströmer

Mario Vargas Llosa

Herta Müller

Jean-Marie Gustave Le Clézio

Doris Lessing

Orhan Pamuk

Harold Pinter

Elfriede Jelinek

J. M. Coetzee

Imre Kertész

V. S. Naipaul

Gao Xingjian

Günter Grass

José Saramago

Dario Fo

Wislawa Szymborska

Seamus Heaney

Kenzaburo Oe

Toni Morrison

Derek Walcott

Nadine Gordimer

Octavio Paz

Camilo José Cela

Naguib Mahfouz

Joseph Brodsky

Wole Soyinka

*Want to discover other award-winning authors and books? You might start with the **National Book Awards** (www.nationalbook.org), which are presented annually to American authors in fiction, nonfiction, poetry, and young people's literature. The **Man Booker Prize** (www.themanbookerprize.com) is awarded for the best original full-length novel written in English and published in the United Kingdom.*

Recent Pulitzer Prizewinners

Recent Pulitzer Prizewinners in Fiction are listed below. For more information on the Pulitzer Prize, visit www.pulitzer.org.

- ❑ *The Sympathizer* . . . . Viet Thanh Nguyen
- ❑ *All the Light We Cannot See* . . . . Anthony Doerr
- ❑ *The Goldfinch* . . . . Donna Tartt
- ❑ *The Orphan Master's Son* . . . . Adam Johnson
- ❑ *A Visit from the Goon Squad* . . . . Jennifer Egan
- ❑ *Tinkers* . . . . Paul Harding
- ❑ *Olive Kitteridge* . . . . Elizabeth Strout
- ❑ *The Brief Wondrous Life of Oscar Wao* . . . . Junot Diaz
- ❑ *The Road* . . . . Cormac McCarthy
- ❑ *March* . . . . Geraldine Brooks
- ❑ *Gilead* . . . . Marilynne Robinson
- ❑ *The Known World* . . . . Edward P. Jones
- ❑ *Middlesex* . . . . Jeffrey Eugenides
- ❑ *Empire Falls* . . . . Richard Russo
- ❑ *The Amazing Adventures
      of Kavalier & Clay* . . . . Michael Chabon
- ❑ *Interpreter of Maladies* . . . . Jhumpa Lahiri
- ❑ *The Hours* . . . . Michael Cunningham
- ❑ *American Pastoral* . . . . Philip Roth
- ❑ *Martin Dressler:
      The Tale of an American Dreamer* . . . . Steven Millhauser
- ❑ *Independence Day* . . . . Richard Ford
- ❑ *The Stone Diaries* . . . . Carol Shields

The **PEN/Faulkner Award** (www.penfaulkner.org/award_for_fiction) honors the best published fiction by American citizens. The **National Book Critics Circle Award** (www.bookcritics.org/awards) presents awards for books and reviews published in the United States in fiction, nonfiction, poetry, memoir/autobiography, biography, and criticism. You'll find more information on these and other book awards at www.bookprizeinfo.com.

Among the World's Great Books . . .

Fiction

❏ *The Adventures of Huckleberry Finn* . . . . Mark Twain

❏ *Alice's Adventures in Wonderland* . . . . . . Lewis Carroll

❏ *Beloved* . . . . Toni Morrison

❏ *Beowulf* . . . . Author unknown

❏ *Catch-22.* . . . . Joseph Heller

❏ *The Color Purple* . . . . Alice Walker

❏ *The Count of Monte Cristo* . . . . Alexandre Dumas

❏ *Crime and Punishment.* . . . . Fyodor Dostoyevsky

❏ *Don Quixote* . . . . Miguel de Cervantes

❏ *Dracula* . . . . Bram Stoker

❏ *Fahrenheit 451* . . . . Ray Bradbury

❏ *Ficciones* . . . . Jorge Luis Borges

❏ *The Hobbit* . . . . J. R. R. Tolkien

❏ *The House of the Seven Gables* . . . . Nathaniel Hawthorne

❏ *The House of the Spirits.* . . . . Isabel Allende

❏ *Independent People.* . . . . Halldór Laxness

❏ *Invisible Man.* . . . . Ralph Ellison

❏ *Jane Eyre* . . . . Charlotte Brontë

❏ *Journey to the West.* . . . . Wu Cheng'en

❏ *Kokoro* . . . . Natsume Sōseki

❏ *Le Morte d'Arthur* . . . . Sir Thomas Malory

❏ *Les Misérables* . . . . Victor Hugo

❏ *Lord Jim* . . . . Joseph Conrad

❏ *The Maltese Falcon* . . . . Dashiell Hammett

❏ *The Metamorphosis* . . . . Franz Kafka

❏ *Middlemarch.* . . . . George Eliot

❏ *Moby-Dick* . . . . Herman Melville

❏ *Nineteen Eighty-Four* . . . . George Orwell

❏ *The Odyssey* . . . . Homer

❏ *The Old Man and the Sea* . . . . Ernest Hemingway

- ☐ *One Day in the Life of Ivan Denisovich* . Aleksandr Solzhenitsyn
- ☐ *One Hundred Years of Solitude* . . . . Gabriel García Márquez
- ☐ *The Picture of Dorian Gray* . . . . Oscar Wilde
- ☐ *Pride and Prejudice* . . . . Jane Austen
- ☐ *Slaughterhouse-Five* . . . . Kurt Vonnegut
- ☐ *The Sound and the Fury* . . . . William Faulkner
- ☐ *A Tale of Two Cities* . . . . Charles Dickens
- ☐ *Their Eyes Were Watching God* . . . . Zora Neale Hurston
- ☐ *To Kill A Mockingbird* . . . . Harper Lee
- ☐ *Treasure Island* . . . . Robert Louis Stevenson
- ☐ *The Turn of the Screw* . . . . Henry James
- ☐ *Twenty Thousand Leagues Under the Sea* . . Jules Verne
- ☐ *Walden* . . . . Henry David Thoreau
- ☐ *War and Peace* . . . . Leo Tolstoy
- ☐ *The War of the Worlds* . . . . H. G. Wells
- ☐ *Wuthering Heights* . . . . Emily Brontë

Nonfiction

- ☐ *Arctic Dreams* . . . . Barry Lopez
- ☐ *Blue Highways* . . . . William Least Heat-Moon
- ☐ *A Brief History of Time* . . . . Stephen Hawking
- ☐ *Bully for Brontosaurus* . . . . Stephen Jay Gould
- ☐ *Bury My Heart at Wounded Knee* . . . . . . Dee Brown
- ☐ *The Diary of a Young Girl* . . . . Anne Frank
- ☐ *Endurance* . . . . Alfred Lansing
- ☐ *The Fabric of the Cosmos* . . . . Brian Greene
- ☐ *The Fire Next Time* . . . . James Baldwin
- ☐ *Guns, Germs, and Steel* . . . . Jared Diamond
- ☐ *The Hero with a Thousand Faces* . . . . . . Joseph Campbell
- ☐ *I Know Why the Caged Bird Sings* . . . . . . Maya Angelou
- ☐ *In Cold Blood* . . . . Truman Capote
- ☐ *Incidents in the Life of a Slave Girl* . . . . . Harriet Jacobs
- ☐ *The Innocents Abroad* . . . . Mark Twain

- [ ] *Kon-Tiki* . . . . Thor Heyerdahl
- [ ] *The Lives of a Cell* . . . . Lewis Thomas
- [ ] *Me Talk Pretty One Day* . . . . David Sedaris
- [ ] *Midnight in the Garden of Good and Evil* John Berendt
- [ ] *Night* . . . . Elie Wiesel
- [ ] *Out of Africa* . . . . Isak Dinesen
- [ ] *Pilgrim at Tinker Creek* . . . . Annie Dillard
- [ ] *The Perfect Storm* . . . . Sebastian Junger
- [ ] *The Prince* . . . . Niccolò Machiavelli
- [ ] *A Room of One's Own* . . . . Virginia Woolf
- [ ] *A Short History of Nearly Everything* . . . . Bill Bryson
- [ ] *Silent Spring* . . . . Rachel Carson
- [ ] *The Snow Leopard* . . . . Peter Matthiessen
- [ ] *The Souls of Black Folk* . . . . W. E. B. Du Bois
- [ ] *The Travels of Marco Polo* . . . . Rustichello da Pisa
  . . . . & Marco Polo
- [ ] *The Voyage of the Beagle* . . . . Charles Darwin
- [ ] *West with the Night* . . . . Beryl Markham
- [ ] *Wind, Sand, and Stars* . . . . Antoine de Saint-Exupéry
- [ ] *A Year in Provence* . . . . Peter Mayle

Drama

Attention must be paid to drama as well. Here are a few great plays to get you started:

- [ ] *Arsenic and Old Lace* . . . . Joseph Kesselring
- [ ] *The Cherry Orchard* . . . . Anton Chekhov
- [ ] *Death of a Salesman* . . . . Arthur Miller
- [ ] *A Doll's House* . . . . Henrik Ibsen
- [ ] *Faust* . . . . Johann Wolfgang von Goethe
- [ ] *Glengarry Glen Ross* . . . . David Mamet
- [ ] *Hamlet* . . . . William Shakespeare
- [ ] *The Importance of Being Earnest* . . . . . . Oscar Wilde
- [ ] *Long Day's Journey into Night* . . . . Eugene O'Neill
- [ ] *A Midsummer Night's Dream* . . . . William Shakespeare

❏ Medea	Euripides
❏ The Mousetrap	Agatha Christie
❏ Oedipus Rex	Sophocles
❏ Our Town	Thornton Wilder
❏ Pygmalion	George Bernard Shaw
❏ A Raisin in the Sun	Lorraine Hansberry
❏ A Streetcar Named Desire	Tennessee Williams
❏ Tartuffe	Molière
❏ Waiting for Godot	Samuel Beckett

Poetry

Are you averse to verse? More disposed toward prose? Don't think you're able to "get" poetry? Fear not. As Plato said, even "poets utter great and wise things which they do not themselves understand." Let this modest potpourri of poets help acquaint you with the "art of substantiating shadows" (Edmund Burke).

Dante Alighieri	John Keats
Matsuo Bashō	Audre Lorde
William Blake	John Milton
Lord Byron	Pablo Neruda
Geoffrey Chaucer	Sylvia Plath
Samuel Taylor Coleridge	Edgar Allan Poe
Billy Collins	Rainer Maria Rilke
Emily Dickinson	Anne Sexton
Stephen Dunn	Richard Siken
T. S. Eliot	Wallace Stevens
Robert Frost	Dylan Thomas
Langston Hughes	Walt Whitman
Kobayashi Issa	William Butler Yeats

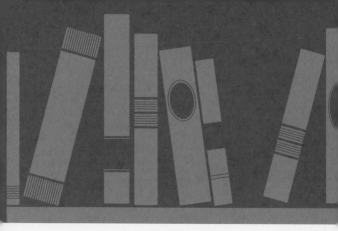

*Outside of a dog, a book
is man's best friend. Inside of a
dog it's too dark to read.*

GROUCHO MARX

MY READING LIFE
My life with books

This is your place to note all your reading favorites, from memorable author events to the books you'd like to have if you were stranded on a desert island!

Favorite Books

Favorite Authors

Memorable Book and Author Events

When audiences come to see us authors lecture, it is largely in the hope that we'll be funnier to look at than to read.

SINCLAIR LEWIS

Books that Changed My Life

Literary Places I'd Like to Visit

My Childhood Favorites

Books I Liked as a Teen

Books I Liked in College

Favorite Poets and Poems

Books I Was Supposed to Read and Didn't (but still might!)

Favorite Book-related Publications, Shows, Blogs, and Web sites

Books Onscreen

My favorite movies adapted from books

Films based on books that I'd remake

How I'd make it different

Books that would make great movies

Casting notes

Books I'd Like with Me if I Were Stranded on a Desert Island